HOW TO KEEP FROM GETTING FIRED

HOW TO KEEP FROM GETTING FIRED

**AUREN URIS
and
JACK TARRANT**

Henry Regnery Company · Chicago

Library of Congress Cataloging in Publication Data

Uris, Auren.
  How to keep from getting fired.

  1. Success.   2. Employee competitive behavior.
I. Tarrant, John, J., joint author.   II. Title.
HF5386.U715 1975   650'.14   75–19413
ISBN 0-8092-8161-9
ISBN 0-8092-8143-0 pbk.

Published by Henry Regnery Company
180 North Michigan Avenue, Chicago, Illinois 60601
Manufactured in the United States of America
Library of Congress Catalog Card Number: 75–19413
International Standard Book Number: 0-8092-8161-9 (cloth)
                                    0-8092-8143-0 (paper)

Published simultaneously in Canada by
Fitzhenry & Whiteside Limited
150 Lesmill Road
Don Mills, Ontario M3B 2T5
Canada

Contents

Acknowledgments

To all of those people whose expressed concerns for security and livelihood alerted us to the importance of writing this book at this time—our thanks.

And for assistance in the preparation and production of the manuscript, we are grateful to Doris Horvath, Winifred Mathie, Louise Ligato, and Louise Trenta, and also to Beth Harding, Ellen Taylor, and Fay Rossi.

For research in the form of library services, Mary McKenna Summers and Inese Miller of the Research Institute library were especially helpful.

Auren Uris
Jack Tarrant

1

Who Can Benefit
From This Book?

THE ideas, information, and insights of this book have helped thousands of people strengthen their grip on their jobs, increase their promotability, and win peace of mind.

Of course, there are people whose positions with their company are about as secure as anything can be in this world. But if you're not the son of the founder, or are not absolutely indispensable, a do-nothing attitude can be harmful. The individual who becomes complacent may be in for a shock if others in the organization have made efforts to improve their situations. If the crunch should come and an employer may have to decide to furlough people, the employee who has taken steps to strengthen his situation will always have an advantage.

It goes almost without saying that the steps you use to reinforce yourself in your job are precisely those that make you a more valuable employee, with greater potential for growth and better prospects for advancement.

Jobholder Alert

In this book you will find ideas, information, procedures, and approaches that will help you keep, and prosper in, your present job.

Special note: This book isn't a primer on how to find a *new* job. Dozens of helpful books have been written on this subject. Jack Tarrant, in his recent *Getting Fired*, has produced one of the better ones. Actually this book was conceived when Tarrant noticed that in his public appearances in connection with *Getting Fired*, the question he got most often—on "hot lines" when he was on radio and TV—went something like this: "Mr. Tarrant, your talk about job hunting is very interesting, but my problem is different. I *have* a job. What I want to know is, how can I hold on to it?"

It's to the millions of jobholders in the country who suffer feelings of job insecurity that the suggestions in this book are directed. The worry people feel about holding on to their jobs, of course, has been triggered or intensified by the bumpy economic weather that started back in 1973. Scare headlines of layoffs, of companies closing their doors, made people question the financial stability of their employers, and the possible implications for themselves.

Two Key Intensifiers

Two factors loom large in judging the importance of keeping your present job—age and obligations. They bear heavily on your mind when you're assessing your job situation.

The young are often full of optimism and careless of risk. The individual who is just starting his career may not worry much about hanging on to his present position. He is more interested in opportunity. If the opportunity opens up in his present situation, fine. If he loses his job, he has the rosy view that he will get another one fast—and that it's apt to be better.

As we get older we lose some of this resilience. It's a fact of nature. We don't have the bounce we used to have, and we are not as able to handle the stresses—emotional as well as financial—of being out of work. So we are more inclined than we used to be to settle for what we've got, and to try to stay where we are.

Then, too, as we move along in life we give "hostages to fortune." The individual who has mouths to feed cannot be as carefree about getting fired as the person who is still going it alone. An employee may feel personally that he doesn't give a damn whether he loses the job or not. But he has obligations. He has a home to pay off and kids to raise. He must curtail in some way the hot and smoky dreams of youth to conform with the realities of making a steady living. Often it takes considerable moral courage to do this, to make the compromises, sometimes distasteful ones, that are necessary to staying in a job.

How Big Is the Job in Your Scheme of Things?

Then there are other people, often younger, who don't have dependents and who would not feel the world has crashed around them if the job dries up. But they have things to do. They have a lifestyle to pursue, interests that have nothing to do with work. The job is necessary simply as a source of money. That being the case, these people are looking for ways to hang on to that steady paycheck simply as a way of maintaining themselves.

What Else Is There?

When good jobs are plentiful, people don't worry so much about being fired. But when things are tight, it becomes far more important to use a certain amount of planning and ingenuity to stay employed. Even the person who is dissatisfied with his job, and who would like to move, will not welcome involuntary unemployment when there do not seem to be any good jobs to move to.

So there are people to whom the job is an absolute necessity. There are people for whom the job is a source of money that makes a lifestyle possible. There are people who may not find the present situation ideal but who regard it as far preferable to being out of work.

The strategies in this book are addressed to anyone and everyone who wants to hang on to a job because it's a good job or the paycheck is essential or both.

What If My Company Is Having Trouble Staying Alive?

If a company is in deep trouble or is forced out of business, can anything be done to assure the employee's job situation? Of course not. When an organization goes under, every employee—from the president down—loses out.

Is that a likelihood? Yes, but only for some *few companies* and some employees. Statistically, companies that lose the fight for survival are only a tiny percentage of American business and industry. And this same fact pertains in the government sector as well. In 1975 thousands of municipal, state, and federal employees were laid off. But here, too, the percentage was just a fraction of the total. In short, *the odds favor your holding on to your job.*

Two things can prevent people from getting a clear picture of where they stand:

• *Too much ego.* "They can't do without me!" says Paul Chambers. He thinks he's a hotshot and believes everyone else thinks so, too. His inflated self-image matches the Goodyear blimp in size and solidity. What's his opinion based on? Certainly not on hard evidence. He feels he's got people charmed by his manner and wit. Actually his co-workers are pretty much on to him and just play along to avoid hurting his feelings. He might very well be the first to go.

• *Too much humility.* Maggie Marsh is a self-effacing, un-self-confident whizbang. She works in an accounting office, and can straighten out ball-ups, in minutes, that even stump her boss. "If she ever quits," her boss says, "this department will never be the same." And Maggie's view? She gets upset every time she hears of someone getting fired—even if it's on the other side of the continent—because she thinks, "There but for the grace of God. . . ." She couldn't be more wrong about her situation.

Everyone reading this book will emerge not only with specific helps, but perhaps even with a broad-gauge program for job "insurance" and advancement.

Are You Sure You Want to Stick?

One more preliminary: a question you may want to ask yourself. It may seem far-out, but for some people it's worthwhile asking and still more worthwhile answering. We know you're reading this book to learn how to improve your prospects with your present employer. This should mean you set considerable store by the job and what it brings you in security and a steady flow of cash. But take the time to consider this question:

"Am I getting enough out of my job both in cash and satisfaction to *want* to stay with it?"

A pointless question? Not necessarily. Even when jobs are hard to get it may be unwise to stick with a job you really detest. Sure it's OK on a temporary basis. But if you really hate the work you're doing, you have no prospects and the job drains you day by day, and getting through the week from Monday to Friday is an ordeal, you'd be wise to do two things:

• Consider the possibility that what you *really* want is only to hold on to your present job until you can find a better one.

• If you *do* decide that the sooner you change jobs the better off you'll be financially, emotionally, and career-wise, then do what you have to do to insure your job just long enough to land a more desirable replacement. If you want to explore this question, the quiz below can help you do a little self-analysis and come up with a realistic action goal. But if you're satisfied with where you're at and just want to stay there, skip the quiz and go on to the next chapter. —

Rate Your Job Satisfaction

		Yes	Doubtful	No
1.	Are you interested and involved in your day-to-day work?	—	—	—
2.	Let's take that a step further: are you enthusiastic about your daily work?	—	—	—
3.	Do you often find yourself telling your family or friends about some particularly interesting aspect of your work?	—	—	—
4.	Do you plan and organize your work so as to do it faster and more efficiently?	—	—	—
5.	Have you ever thought, "Other people refer to their work as a rat race. I'm glad mine isn't like that"?	—	—	—

6. Do you feel that your work is worthwhile, and that it has a commendable purpose (other than the financial aspect)? — — —

7. Do you spend nonworking time thinking about some unfinished task or an intriguing work problem? — — —

8. Do you feel your job gives you satisfactory status with friends and neighbors? √ — —

9. Would you say you're growing in your job? X — —

10. Do you find it easy to get out of bed in the morning to go to work? — — —

To rate the satisfaction you're getting from your daily job, give yourself *10* points for each Yes, *3* points for each Doubtful, and *0* points for each No. Then rate your numerical score on the scale below:

91 to 100	Face up to the fact: You love your work.
81 to 90	You're getting a fair amount of enjoyment from your work.
71 to 80	Your job is OK—just about.
Below 70	Unfortunately you're not getting satisfaction from your daily work. Should you consider it as "temporary" employment—to have and to hold until you can come up with something better?

In thinking about yourself and your job, one bit of wisdom from people who for one reason or another have done their fair share of job hopping: There is no such thing as a perfect job. Every kind of employment has advantages and disadvantages. We're just suggesting that if the balance is so strongly tipped toward the negative, your strongest bid for job security *and* satisfaction should lead you to consider a job change. And, of course, if and when the job change is made, then all the matters discussed in the pages that follow will apply to the new employer who has been fortunate enough to secure your services.

2

Seven Ways to Make Yourself Indispensable

In this chapter we're going to talk about the stuff of which—for jobholders—dreams are made.

Ah, to be indispensable, to be so necessary to the operation of your company that *it can't get along without you*. . . .

We know the concept is a dream because we've been told repeatedly, "No one is indispensable." And that fact certainly seems to be firmly rooted in business experience:

Helen Begley, office manager of Rexine Products, comes to retirement age. Her boss tries to persuade her to stay: "Helen, you know how much we depend on you here. How about staying on for another year or two?"

But Helen, who has been wisely planning her retirement for several years, has her mind made up: "I'm sorry, Mr. Avery. Of course I'm pleased that you want me to stay on, but I've already made plans to move out West. And Janet is perfectly capable of taking over. . . ."

Helen Begley leaves and, to Mr. Avery's pleasant surprise, Janet Hayes takes over the job of managing the office and does a perfectly good job, in some ways even better than the one that Helen Begley turned in.

And, of course, people quit, or move away, or die. Even people at the very top, where indispensability is supposed to be a more common quality, pass out of the picture and the organization continues to operate and flourish.

What Indispensability Means

Nevertheless you can do a great deal to make yourself so outstandingly important to the operation of your organization that the company would be the loser if you were to leave for whatever reason. Here are six moves you can make to gain that desirable status. By no coincidence at all, these same moves can also brighten your prospects in your organization, put you in line for salary increases, promotion, and so on. Here are the opportunities:

1. *Be the best*. The first, and in some ways the simplest, move to make is to master your own job. Consider Peter Fales in action: Peter is a video-tape editor, one of three editors working for a post-production house that helps prepare TV commercials for broadcasting. Peter is the newest addition to the staff, but he decides he's not going to be low man on the totem pole. He starts his own one-man training program. From the manufacturer of the video-editing equipment he gets all the technical and sales brochures available, to fill out his knowledge of the machines. Then he makes a point of volunteering for the tough assignments, the dogs the other editors scorn, but from which he can learn a good deal. He also puts in as much overtime as possible, not only for the extra income, but to increase his total of operating hours and experience. In six months he's the best operator of his group. When there's a headache or hang-up, his boss comes to him. The

company will now hesitate to fire him. While union regulations require firing by seniority, they may even keep an extra man on the payroll just to hold on to the insurance—that is, assurance—that having Peter around would represent.

2. *Master a related specialty.* In some cases there are tasks or areas of responsibility that, while not directly a part of your job, do impinge on it. By taking steps to become active in these peripheral areas, you can get the attention and high regard that can be crucial. Note Irene Beck's experience:

Irene Beck is a secretary, one of eight, who works for a management-consulting company. The firm is retained by corporate clients suffering from any number of business ailments, which one way or another prevent them from operating smoothly or profitably as their top executives feel they should.

After the firm has made its study and analysis, a report is submitted to the client company, explaining the findings at length, and appropriate recommendations for action.

Now these reports were typed by all the secretaries, including Irene Beck. But after the typing there was an additional step. This was packaging the report for the client's eyes, which meant not only putting the pages into an elegant leather binder but adding finished charts, graphs, and other similar kinds of artwork.

One day the studio that the firm used to do the artwork flubbed it and fouled up two of the diagrams. And the report was due at the client's office in a few hours.

"I think I can fix those up in less time than it would take to send them back to the studio," said Irene.

She went down to the art supply store across the street, got the few things needed, and proceeded to redo the diagrams.

"Great," her boss said. "You're a lifesaver!"

"How about letting me do the charts and other artwork on all the reports?"

"Can you handle it?"

"I'm sure I can." Actually most of the artwork was quite simple, well within the scope of the one year of drafting Irene Beck had taken in school.

In effect Irene had promoted herself. Certainly she now had an edge over the other secretaries, in terms of her flexibility and use to the company. One thing's for sure, if the secretarial group were trimmed down for whatever reason, Irene would now be one of the last to go. She was not only a great convenience—the artwork was done on the spot without having to depend on an outside source—but also she was saving the firm cold, hard cash—a double virtue hard to overlook.

3. *Master "nine jobs."* Bruce Miller found a way to make himself as close to being indispensable as anyone can be. Here is his story:

Recently hired as an editor for a large book publisher, he found himself one of six young hopefuls—all of about the same status as he was. After five or six months spent getting his feet on solid ground and learning the ABC's of his job, he decided he was ready to think of the future. His plan was simple. He set out to learn as much as he could about the many activities that *related to* his work. Here are the specific moves he made:

He took a course in typography in a local commercial art school to learn about type styles, page layout, and so on.

He read up on paper manufacture and paper quality.

He made visits to print shops around town. While few of them printed books, he was able to pick up considerable information that helped him understand some of the problems involved in book production.

He was able to get his boss to arrange for a one-day visit

to a book bindery that his company used. He got to understand some of the processes and problems involved in putting a hardcover binding on a book. He also learned the basics of paperbound books and why the costs between hardcover and paper were so different.

Finally he took a short course in accounting so he could understand the dollars and cents of the publishing business. All this information he had seldom pertained directly to his work, which was reading and editing book manuscripts. But in conversations with his boss and other executives, his know-how from time to time came into a conversation and eventually the full range of his background and education clearly established him as one of the most versatile, best-informed and broadest-gauged editors of the group.

Every job has a number of activities or areas of knowledge that relate to it. A person running a press, for example, can study electric motors, machine mechanics and equipment design, and one way or another be able to use this knowledge in his job. Obviously the same education and learning that expands one's field of knowledge can be used to improve job performance and to increase the possibility of advancement.

One hazard to avoid: In some cases acquiring additional knowledge or skill may impinge on the jobs or areas of responsibility of other people. To make sure you don't step on toes or upset people who think you're trying to "advance over their dead bodies," be circumspect both in the way you go about acquiring information or know-how and the way you use it in strengthening your own position.

Mastering many "trades" can give your job life as many chances as a cat is supposed to have. For cats it's a myth; for you it can't miss.

4. *Be a "keeper of the keys."* In every organization there are certain activities, sometimes directly related to com-

pany operations, sometimes a part of company life but not directly in line with its basic function. For example, many organizations have recreation programs—it may be anything from chess playing during lunch to full-fledged teams—basketball, baseball, bowling, etc. In other instances the activity is a kind of social expression of company life, such as an annual picnic, for example. People who are alert to the opportunities of this type of activity can really give themselves a leg up. Note Al Berry hard at work:

Berry works for a plastics company in a New Jersey suburb. The company has an interesting history. Years ago, before it was acquired as a subsidiary of a larger company, it used to be in the business of manufacturing consumer products using an early plastic made of cellulose nitrate. In those days the company products showed up in practically every home in the country. Brush and comb sets, picture frames, decorative pieces, yes, and even men's collars were made of the material.

Al Berry set out to collect as much of the company memorabilia as he could. At home he set up glass cabinets containing examples of the work that his company used to do—articles about the material, advertising, any bits of history about the company, of its people immediately found a place in his library.

It became known that the company was going to have an anniversary celebration. Al Berry contacted the personnel director and described his collection of company products and lore.

"Great," said the personnel director. "If you will cooperate, we'll set up your collection as one of the major attractions."

The exhibition was one of the hits of the occasion, and overnight, Al Berry became the "company historian." This special status set him apart and clearly "above" his peers. In human terms Al Berry was as much a fixture in the company as the foundation stone, and the job became almost as secure.

In many organizations there are opportunities for alert and interested employees to develop a special position for themselves. Even if it's unofficial—as was Al Berry's company historian designation—it makes one a very special employee likely to get very special consideration.

Here are some other possible areas in which you can become a company "specialist":

History of the physical area in which your company is located. ("You see Building A over there?" says a self-made expert, "that's where the main house of the farm was located that used to occupy this property.")

Become knowledgeable in the community life in which the company is located. "The volunteer firemen need a new fire engine," Christine Albert tells her boss. "I think it would help the company in our community relations if we got involved in the fund raising for that purpose."

Her boss passes the word along to the front office, and Christine's astuteness is duly noted and approved.

5. *Is there a new "ground floor"?* People who start with an organization that newly enters the business lists are said to be in on the ground floor, and there's usually an advantage of being a charter member of an organization. One's own prospects and career intermingle with the growth of the company. Success stories of this kind are endless. People who had menial jobs in organizations that eventually became giants—IBM, Xerox, you name them—ended up being department heads, executives, even major stockholders. But only a certain number of people can be in at the beginning. However, for many more the opportunity is repeated at a later date. Consider the happy experience of Paula Berne:

Paula Berne was one of fifteen employees who operated a forming press for J. T. Ryan Plastics. One day she heard from the grapevine that the company was starting a new venture, forming large sheets of clear plastic into windshields for small boats. Her boss, Harry Burke, was going to be in charge of the pilot operation. She talked to Harry about it, and learned that he was going to need two people for the new job. She asked to be assigned, and Burke said OK.

Once the work started Paula got kidded unmercifully by her co-workers. For one thing the forming was being done in an old garage on the back lot. "How's Siberia?" she was asked. And one jokester came up with, "I understand they put one of your windows in an outboard runabout and it sank."

But Paula stuck to the assignment and helped Burke get the kinks out of new process. Eventually a large production order came in. Four more people were assigned to the windshield operation. And since Burke had to spend most of his time back at the regular forming presses, he needed an assistant to take charge while he was away. Paula was the logical choice.

As long as J. T. Ryan Plastics got windshield orders, Paula's job was secure. And note that her changed situation not only got her a promotion and higher pay but also increased her flexibility—she had the know-how for two different operations—to say nothing about getting her foot on the first rung of the supervisory ladder.

As happened at the plastics company, organizations often start a new activity. It may be a new line, such as the boat windshields. It may be an entirely new product that takes the company into unfamiliar areas of production and selling. Sometimes the new "ground floor" shows up as a new plant, or department.

Each innovation, each departure of this kind, creates opportunities. People are needed to supervise, to operate the facilities. And the employee who is on the alert for such developments can, like Paula Berne, improve her lot considerably.

6. *Learn something crucial.* Every business has aspects of its operation that are "sensitive," that are not for public knowledge. In many cases it's not the public that concerns the organization, but the possibility of a competitor becoming privy to the information that is of concern.

One way of making yourself a "tough employee to fire" is to work yourself into a spot that gives you access to this vital material. For example:

Bob David was a production foreman working for the Rex Moore Molding Company. Chief product of the firm was advertising displays, made of an inexpensive woodlike plastic. The exact ingredients and proportions of the plastic were kept secret by Mr. Moore, who had been trained as a chemical engineer, and was the developer both of the formulas and the exact methods by which the material was formed in large bronze molds.

As the business improved two things happened: First, Rex Moore had to spend more time outside, calling on customers and selling new prospects. And more batches of plastic had to be mixed to fill the increasing number of orders.

Originally, Mr. Moore had been able to supervise all the mixing himself. A workman weighed and dumped the major ingredients into the hopper that fed into the mixing machines. Then Moore had the man leave the mixing room, and he added the plasticizers and the catalytic agent that gave the material special strength and molding quality.

Bob David saw the problem being created by Moore's being the only one to know the formulas. And once, when Moore had to come rushing back to the shop to prepare a mix for the presses, which were standing idle for lack of material, Bob David suggested that someone else had better be trained to supervise the mixing:

"And I don't mind telling you, boss," he said, "I was an A student in high school chemistry."

Moore nodded. "You win on both points, Bob. Stay after work tonight, and I'll start breaking you in."

By his alertness to the situation Bob had gotten his toe in the door before either of his two fellow foremen had even spotted the opportunity. And now that he was privy to the special formulas used by the company, he had put himself in a special category. The Rex Moore Molding Company would have to be in a pretty desperate situation before his name would be considered for ex-employee status.

The Law's the Limit

However, there's one aspect to the Bob David case history you must watch out for. Although Bob David now knew the secret formulas, he was not altogether free to pass along this information in ways that would do damage to the company.

While there's some fogginess as to what constitutes a trade secret, in general the courts frown upon an employee's unfair use of secret knowledge obtained in the course of his work. Of course Bob David's strengthened grip on his job lay in the fact that an employer doesn't even want to risk the possibility of having such vital information get into unfriendly hands. As long as Bob David is an employee, he has good reason to loyally protect company interests. If he's asked to leave before he wants to, his knowledge becomes a threat.

Some people think that unless there's a written agreement between employee and company that prevents the employee from passing along company secrets, there's no restriction. But this is not the case. Stated simply an employee has a common-law duty not to divulge trade secrets acquired during his employment, and it is not necessary that there be any agreement not to reveal them.

In casing your own organization for areas that it might be wise for you to win the privilege of working in, remember that a company's secrets need not be limited to technical data, such as formulas, special ingredients, and so on. It might be the design or use of a novel device or process not known to the public generally. Or, it can be information compiled with a great expenditure of time and money, such as a list of customers, market studies of an intensive or extensive nature, development on products or processes, and so on.

By getting in on the inside of such special information areas of your company's operation you become a key man, automatically passed over when the pruning shears go over the personnel lists.

7. *Make a major contribution to profitability.* In 1969 Charlene Friend worked as a writer for a company that produced training materials for industry and the government. The materials usually took the form of printed case histories that were read by trainees in management who then discussed the cases in meetings. To make the meetings as productive as possible, the leader was provided with a handbook that helped him direct the discussions toward productive channels.

A few years after Charlene got her job, competition in the field had increased to the point where sales were really tough, and as volume fell belt tightening became the order of the day. Eventually one of the six staff writers was fired. Clearly the job prospects of the other five were shaky.

At this point Charlene Friend went to her boss with a suggestion: "Mr. Baker, it seems to me that in order to stay afloat we've got to come up with something new and different that will give us an edge over the competitors. Here's an idea I'd like you to consider. Suppose that instead of printing our case histories material we record it on tape, you know, the small cassettes that by now are all over the place. Now, although tape programs aren't unique, I have a couple of new wrinkles to suggest. Once we go on tape we're then in a position to include in the package a preliminary talk on each one of our training subjects by an outstanding expert in the field as a kickoff to the meeting. . . ."

Charlene Friend went on to add a few additional features: suggestions to the conference leader to play back key sections of the case as they come up for discussion. In some cases a recording of the discussion itself so that sections could be replayed in case of disagreements over what had been said, and so on.

Tom Baker was interested in the idea but hesitated to invest in what was essentially a new product when funds were so low. Eventually he felt he had no alternative. Kill or cure, he decided, and started a crash project to get a pilot program going. Needless to say Charlene Friend was leader of the task force. Within four months' time the program was test-marketed and it became clear at once that customers were eager to buy in order to add the element of freshness to training programs that traditionally tend to wear down because of monotony and boredom.

Charlene Friend became the firm's hero. Not only had she strengthened her position in the company but had actually revitalized the organization itself—a double gain.

There's an old saying in business that "Ideas don't care who has them." Behind this bit of business lore is the idea that a sound idea may originate at the grass roots as well as at the top. And every organization can profit from ideas. Thousands of firms actually develop complex suggestion systems to induce employees to hitch their brainpower to the company wagon.

No matter where you are in your organization, you undoubtedly can improve operations, cut costs, and make other worthwhile contributions by making constructive suggestions. But the kind of ideas that can really make a major difference in your situation are basic ones that will score an obvious improvement in company profitability. There's no limit to the aspects of organizational activity that can benefit from a sound idea. Some of the possibilities include new products, improvements in basic methods of operation, new markets, new types of packaging. In one case an employee became a company hero by suggesting a new way to sell a company product. His firm, which produced costume jewelry, usually sold to department and novelty concerns. Jack French, one of the company designers, went to his boss one day and said, "Bert, how would it be if we designed a special line that we could sell direct to the consumer by mail order?" Eventually sales by mail became a major source of profit for the firm.

Of course basic ideas that can improve the fortunes of a business concern don't come easy. As a matter of fact there is usually an ongoing competition among employees to come up with such ideas. Everyone from the errand boy to the president is in the swim.

But the point that many people are unaware of is that it isn't necessary to sit and wait for an idea to come your way. You can stimulate your thinking. These three steps can help:

A.   Be continually on the alert. Train yourself to be idea-minded. As much as you can, direct your thinking toward the *production* of ideas.

B.   Focus your thinking. Brainpower can seldom get revved up in a vacuum. To sharpen your thinking direct it toward company operations, starting with those that are most familiar to you. Try to think through the answers to such questions as, How could that be done differently? Is there any new technology that could be used? (Essentially that was the question that Charlene Friend asked in order to come up with the concept of the taped program.)

C.   Are there organizations doing things that we can adapt or parallel? People who study business organizations constantly comment on their rigidity. "There's always a tendency to fall into ruts and stay there," says one management consultant. "This often prevents a firm from making a slight change that would help it considerably, whether it's a matter of moving into a new sales territory or changing one of its product lines."

By studying what other companies do, how they produce, what they produce, where they sell, how they sell, you may come up with an approach that can make your company more successful—and you along with it.

3

You and Your Company—
How Are You Set?

Let's zero in directly on your job situation. There are key questions that provide a useful picture. For example, the number of years you've been with your company is a factor. The kind of work you do is another, and so on. Once you assess your situation, you're in a better position to move ahead because you have a clearer background and a better perspective on where you're at.

By getting a straightforward view of your employment situation, it's possible to clarify the answer to a key question: How strong—or weak—is your grip on your job right now?

Consider the obvious difference in the job security of these two people:

• Jay Hunt has been with his company, a manufacturer of housewares, for fifteen years. He's well liked and is an important cog in the organizational machinery. But the hitch is, his company is having a really tough time of it, and

if the creditors aren't willing to make concessions, the
company may have to close down. If that happens, despite
his employer's wishes to the contrary, Jay will join the job-
hunting brigade.

• Tom Locke is equally valued as an employee by his
organization, but Locke's firm, which rents trucks, is
operating profitably and has a bright future. Presumably,
so does Tom.

To check the foundations of your job security, the
keystone on which it rests, let's consider these two basic
questions in turn: How solid is your organization? How well
are you fixed in it?

Rating Your Company

There are a number of ways to rate the solidity of an
organization. One way is to look at its profit-and-loss
statement. And profitability of operation is always a major
factor. In recent years measuring the stability or worth of
an organization has been developed to a fairly precise art.
The major impetus of this approach began in the late fifties
when acquisitions and mergers and the forming of
conglomerate companies became a major force on the
business scene.

If you were at the head of Company A and were interested in acquiring Company B as a subsidiary or affiliate,
naturally you'd want to know a good deal about Company
B: How stable it was, what its prospects were, and how
worthy it was of the kind of investment you were considering.

Well, some of the methods of the experts that
businessmen use to check out the viability of an
organization can help you get a line on your own employer.
The questions below are based on your getting information
that is generally available, not only to employees but to the

public at large. Answer them as accurately as you can, and then use the rating procedure to come up with a score. Of course the score is just a rough approximation, but it helps you concretize the thing you're after, the assurance that your employer is at least going to stay in business long enough to employ you as long as you want to adorn its roster.

	Yes	No	Don't Know
1. Is the industry of which your company is a part a growth industry—that is, is it expanding in relation to other types of business? (For example, if your company is making buggy whips, the future might not be too bright. If it's in oil products or energy production, prospects would be considerably brighter.)	—	—	—
2. Is your company growing or expanding—that is, starting up new units, hiring more people, and so on? (Some companies, like individuals, reach a peak, then head downhill. Others are vigorous, still on the way up.)	—	—	—
3. Is your company			
a. increasing its gross annual sales?	—	—	—
b. increasing its annual profits?	—	—	—

    c. adding new products to its
line? — — —
    d. expanding into new market
areas? — — —
    e. in a financially sound
situation as indicated by
its annual statement? — — —
4. Does your company possess
special advantages that give it
an edge over its competitors,
such as
    a. Patents? — — —
    b. Specially designed equipment or facilities? — — —
    c. Secret formulas or other
unique data? — — —
    d. A corps of special experts,
either its management or
technical-scientific staff? — — —
5. Does it have good relations
with its customers—that means
they'll be getting orders as long
as the customers are around to
place them? — — —
6. Are management-employee relations a favorable factor—
management interested in employee welfare, employees
actively pro-company? — — —

Scoring

We suggest that no matter how your organization rates, you
look behind the score for your final assessment. But start, at

least, by adding up the *Yeses* and *Nos*. Every *Yes* is a favorable factor; each *No* suggests an organizational weakness. You may want to check into the areas covered by your *Don't Knows,* and get the information if you can.

It's unlikely that your firm—or any firm—will score 11 yeses. But the more yes answers, generally, the lustier the organization. Review each no answer. What is the overall picture that emerges? Note that some nos are especially bad news. For example, a negative reply to question 5 clearly suggests a shaky connection to the lifeline of business, the marketplace.

Now the reason we say don't take the actual numerical score too seriously is that one single *No* in a crucial area may outweigh a large number of *Yeses.* For example, if the answer about finances (3e) is negative, other indications may lose considerable weight.

The virtue of the questions is that it helps you get an objective picture, takes you away from the usual perspective that comes from your daily contacts with people and activities, that may be either pleasant or otherwise, reassuring or otherwise, but may not really be a good measure of stability.

Now that you've gotten an overview of the state your company is in, you may want to consider the three possibilities—

• *Bright future.* If all the signs and portents are positive, if, as far as objective signs are concerned, your organization is as solid as the Rockies, you can go on to the next point at issue, your own situation as an employee.

• *The signs are mixed.* Where weighing the pros and cons of your company situation results in a so-so conclusion—that is, the company isn't doing well but it's not doing badly, either, and has reasonable prospects for survival—it's probably best to hold this matter in abeyance for the moment and go on to the next consideration, how you fit into the company picture.

In general we would suggest that you stick with an employer that faces a somewhat bumpy road. For one thing, uncertainties of this kind often present opportunities for advancement and promotion for the alert employee. For another, there are very few completely "healthy" business organizations. Even the best-situated ones can have a sudden downturn—remember what happened to those indestructible giants, General Motors and Ford Motor Company, when the bottom dropped out of the automobile market in 1974.

• *There's a wolf at the door.* If, as a result of your survey of your company, you think survival in the immediate future is questionable, then you have to ask yourself a tough question: Would you do better to hold on and go down with the ship, or is it the height of wisdom for you to start looking around for another job?

One thing *not* to do is to resign or give notice that you're intending to leave. Anyone who intends to hit the job market is in a much stronger situation, mentally, financially, and bargaining-wise, if he does his job hunting while still employed.

Now let's turn to the second major element in these considerations: Where do you stand with your company? Just how important are you to the powers that be? If there were to be a 5% personnel cut across the board, would your name be on the list of those to be let go? Where would you be in a 10% cut? 25%?

Perhaps you can't answer questions like these in the abstract. But the considerations below will help give you a useful picture of your situation vis-a-vis your organization.

Your Standing in Your Company

Mike Baum listened to his boss's words and couldn't believe his ears: ". . . and I'm really sorry, Mike. You can be sure if there were any other way to ease the cost pressures, I'd take them. But we've cut everything to the bone. Now the only way we can keep going is to trim personnel. It's no reflection on you personally, of course. It's just that your skills are not in line with our greatest needs right now. . . . Please count on me to help you get another job quickly. I'll do whatever I can. I'm happy to say our separation arrangements will minimize your immediate money worries. . . ."

Mike's boss has supplied one reason why he was picked for dismissal, while half a dozen others doing the same type of work were passed over—the nature of his job skills. But the reasons why A gets the ax while B does not are many. And your zeroing in on them, and seeing whether they do or don't apply to your situation is the second half of the answer to the question of your job security.

How Firm Is Your Hold?

Some people have both the information and the objectivity to be able to describe accurately just what their job situation is. They can say, for example—

"I'll have my job as long as the company stays in business." Or,

"If there were a personnel cut tomorrow I'd be one of the first to go."

But those are the extremes. Most people lie somewhere in the middle. This means they're able to make some firm statements about their situation but are in doubt about others.

In order to clarify the picture you have to put yourself

down on paper, and take a broad overall look that touches most of the bases. This is what will come through when you use the checklist tools that follow.

Words That Tell a Story

Language is a marvelous thing, and the American language is doubly so. "American," by the way, is English enriched by the words and phrases of your common, colorful, earthy talk. For example, when you say a young man is unkempt, sloppily dressed, seems preoccupied by matters beyond the immediate scene, you're using English. When you say, "He's a hippie," you've said a great deal more, and said it in fewer words. That's American.

Our daily speech has many words and phrases that are so vivid, so clear-cut, they can be used as measuring devices. For example, they can tell you where you stand on the job ladder, as far as accomplishment and potential are concerned. Here's a brief sample:

"Fair-haired boy." This is the individual who's going places. Are you one?

"Dead-ender." It doesn't matter how old or young, this person is in a box. Does this describe you?

"Young hopeful." There are aspirations, but as yet no one, neither the person nor the boss, knows whether or not he or she is going to make it. Is this the shoe that fits?

As a first step use the checklist below to assess quickly *how you look to yourself in your present job.* Which term, in your opinion, best describes you?

( ) Fair-haired boy
( ) Dead-ender
( ) Young hopeful
( ) Overeager beaver (You're trying too hard and getting nowhere.)

( ) Heir apparent (You've got it made when the boss retires.)

( ) On the make (You've got plans and intend to implement them.)

( ) A plugger (You work hard but prospects are just so-so.)

Suggest your own term: _____

It's not too important how you come out. Even if you think you're a Fair-haired boy or a Dead-ender, consider this only as a preliminary size-up. You need more information before reaching a conclusion.

The important thing is to start thinking about yourself *objectively*. Once you start this type of self-analysis, the additional measuring tools, about to be supplied, will become more effective.

Now go on to the next step of self-appraisal and remember that this self-assessment has a vital purpose: to help you see yourself and your situation more clearly than you ever did before.

Racking Up Additional Information

Answer the questions below as accurately as you can. Rely on general impressions, of course, because some of the points have to do with your "feel" of a situation. But also, think of specific job situations, incidents, and relationships that can clue you in to the realities.

		Yes	No	Don't Know
1.	Do you feel you are appreciated in your company			
	a. as an individual?	—	—	—
	b. because of the high quality of the work you do?	—	—	—

    c. because of special contri-
butions above and beyond
the call of duty—such as
suggestions, for example?   — —   —

2. In your own opinion, do you
feel you have a good future
with your present employer?   — —   —

3. Are you particularly strong in
your job skills, so that you have
an edge over others doing the
same work?   — —   —

4. Do you have a good working
relationship with your boss?   — —   —

5. Would you say you're known
favorably by people at the top
of your company—either by
personal contact or reputation?   — —   —

6. If you were your boss and got
word to "let 10% of the people
in the department go," would
you surely be among those who
stay?   — —   —

7. Do you have special qualifications or training that make
you a more-valuable-than-
average person to your company?   — —   —

8. If you were fired, could you
walk into the offices of a
competitor and practically be
assured of being hired?   — —   —

How It Adds Up
As before, add up the *Yeses, Nos,* and *Don't Knows.*

Obviously the more *Yeses* you scored, the better off you are. But in a way, the questions answered *No* are more important, because these tip you off to weak areas in which you can take remedial action. For example: Let's say you can't truthfully say the answer to question number 4, "Do you have a good working relationship with your boss?"—is anything but *No*. Once you've pinpointed this fact, it becomes a goal you can start working toward. (Chapters 5 and 6 will provide some solid suggestions to start the process going.)

Or, consider 1c, about special contributions you can make to your company in the form of ideas, suggestions, and so on. If your answer here is in the negative, you can now proceed, with your new awareness of this weak point, to see why you haven't been active in this area, and can step up attempts to score.

Here, too, your *Don't Know* replies are worth further digging. It's quite possible that just the process of investigation can open up possibilities for constructive action that will do your standing in the organization a world of good.

4

How a Company Judges You

W<small>HEN</small> a manager is told, "You have to lay off X number of people from the department," he has a problem. Usually it is a tough one. And in some cases managers have said, "The toughest thing I ever had to do in my life is to fire somebody."

Partly to offset the ordeal of firing, managers try to develop a set of objective standards on which to base the firing decision. These standards are made up of both negative and positive elements. The negative elements are usually easy to identify. For example, here are some of the negative or knock-out factors managers use to pinpoint the employee who is most readily expendable—*the employee who happens to be marked by one or more of these qualities may consider his employment situation as being rather shaky:*

Unessential work. You would think that everything that is done in a company is essential. After all, isn't the firm paying good money in terms of salaries, payroll taxes, fringes, etc., to have it done? But the fact is that organizations, like gardens, become weedy; that is, certain procedures or services develop that may have a purpose, but it is a purpose not essential to the overall operation of the company. For example: The Climax Foundry Company has a good-sized cafeteria for its 400 employees. In plush times the employee who took care of the cafeteria complained that some of the work was too heavy and that the overall job required more than one person could manage. Her boss, head of maintenance, agreed to get her a part-time assistant. When the crunch came it became clear that the affluence that permitted the addition of the part-time cafeteria worker no longer existed to justify the expense. In a cutback, the part-timer was let go.

Similarly there are all kinds of activities in a company that develop when there is plenty of money around. But when the chill winds of business hardship start to blow, the people doing these less-than-essential tasks are prime prospects for a furlough.

Sub-par ability. Another prime prospect for the pink slip is the employee whose job skills are below average. Actually from the company's standpoint the need to cut back has one desirable benefit: The organization now has the opportunity to cut out employee deadwood, the individuals who don't pull their weight.

You have to understand that the average company makes a distinction between a marginal employee who, for one reason or another, can't or doesn't cut the mustard and the employee of long tenure who has been with the company for many years but who, because of advanced age or failing health, just isn't as young and capable as he used to be. Most companies are humane enough to consider the loyal employees whose failing skills represent growing older in the service as members of a group that will receive special consideration.

But for the newer employee whose performance isn't satisfactory, the indications are less favorable. And as we have said, the company uses the need to trim rosters as an occasion for eliminating those who have not been up to snuff. In addition to the two major factors mentioned, add anything that may bring out the firing squad: excessive absenteeism, insubordination, quarrelsomeness, and petty dishonesty.

Aside from knock-out factors, however, the typical employer uses a range of qualities to evaluate employees. In general those who rate high on these desirable qualities have a good hold on their jobs. Those who rate low are less fortunate. Here are elements that you can build into your job performance that can help you come out on top when the company starts measuring employees for the stay-or-go decision.

The Seven Qualities That Make You Look Good

There is a range of things you can do in the course of your day-to-day work that can make you shine like a bright star in the eyes of your employer. With these qualities working for you, you can be sure you've stacked the cards heavily in your favor.

The Seven Lively Virtues

1. Job skill
2. Acceptance of company goals
3. Cost consciousness
4. Work improvement
5. Ideas and problem solving
6. Cooperativeness
7. Growth potential

Now let's look at these one at a time and see where you can make them powerful factors working in your favor:

1.   *Job skill*. Whether you are a secretary, a lathe hand, a computer programmer, or a middle-management executive, your daily work represents a stage on which you can show your stuff.

In some cases you are one of a group of people doing approximately the same kind of work. Let's say for example you are a foreman in an electronics plant and there are half a dozen other department heads at approximately your level. To some extent a measure of your job skill is represented by questions like these:

How good are you compared to your competitors? Are you the best in the group of seven supervisors? Are you somewhere in the middle?

Let's not kid ourselves about one thing: There *can* be a major difference between an employee's actual performance and his reputation as a performer. It can work both ways: Bob Wright is an excellent reporter. He turns in solid pieces that reflect an analytical mind and a fine writing skill. But unfortunately Bob doesn't cut a fine figure on the staff. He is not very aggressive and not very good at blowing his own horn. The result is he is a better performer than he gets credit for.

Lee Artimas on the other hand is thought of as a hotshot reporter. Starting on the newspaper about the same time that Bob Wright did, he has a brassy impressive manner. He has done one or two outstanding stories, which he has parlayed into a superior reputation that somehow disguises a considerable amount of mediocrity.

The point is that there are two aspects to making an employer value your job skills. One is to master them as much as you can. The other is to make the moves that will tactfully build your reputation to match your performance.

How do you do this? Here is the recommendation of one personnel expert: "An employee can do a public relations job for himself in a number of ways. For example, letting his views be heard in meetings or discussions about the work. Talking to his boss and colleagues about some of the finer points of the tasks that arise. Voicing opinions based on past experience, and so on, that back up his point of view and authority."

2.   *Acceptance of company goals.* "The last thing I want to be is a company man," says an engineer. The way he says it you get the impression that he is speaking with personal pride, and especially that you can lose personal integrity by going along with the company establishment.

Actually the phrase *company man* and the hostility toward the concept date back to the bad old days of labor-management conflict.

These days there is a better understanding and acceptance of the idea that there is a strong overlap between company welfare and employee welfare. Often what is good for the company is good for the employee as well.

Of course this doesn't mean that the individual may not have interests that are opposed to those of the company. As a matter of fact nothing makes this clearer than a layoff situation where a company can further its interest for survival by thinning out the employee roster, which creates subsequent difficulties for the employees who are laid off. But it is accepted now that company and employee have many objectives that are identical. The survival of the company, its growth, and, for that matter, the increased capability of the employee are mutually desirable.

The employee who is aware of company objectives—in terms of smooth operating achievement of performance objectives and all—and signals his acceptance of these goals can strengthen his position in the eyes of his employer.

3. *Cost consciousness.* The employee who treats company property as carefully as he would his own, who respectfully "spends" company money for company facilities, equipment, and materials, also takes on a special value to his employer.

4. *Work improvement.* Talk to anyone in management and he will tell you that one of the ongoing efforts of every branch and department of an organization is the improvement of work methods. An order department tries to streamline the methods by which the order is processed. The assembly department in a toy company tries to put together its units a little faster with fewer delays and errors.

Improvements in the work seldom take place with spontaneity. Usually what happens is that an employee figures out a way to do some bit of his work in a somewhat more efficient way. A drill press operator figures out how to drill two parts at a time instead of one. An executive develops a better method for handling his incoming mail and then has more time to spend on other matters.

Your interest in improving the work that you are doing or that is part of your department's operation is another positive quality that your company will view with favor.

5. *Ideas and problem solving.* No matter what kind of job you have, no matter what work you do, there is something else you can produce in connection with your work that will make you look good to your employer. It is simply this: Come up with ideas; come up with solutions to departmental problems. Consider the case of Betty Moore: Betty Moore is a member of a customer-relations department for a book publisher. She handles complaints and related problems for the stores and other book outlets across the country.

One day Betty has an idea that she discusses with her boss: "Mr. Norman, wouldn't it be a good move for us to stop just being a complaint-handling operation? I suggest we survey some of our bigger customers and find out what we can do to improve our services to them. Eventually this should lead to more sales. . . ."

One thing you don't have to worry about: that there will be no problems around for you to tackle. Every company, every department, has problems. And they come in all shapes and sizes. Many of them are obvious to the naked eye. You can see where a pileup of work signals a bottleneck. Perhaps you have an idea of how that situation can be improved. But perhaps you're a member of a unit that's functioning with relative smoothness. In that case it may not be your eyes but your ears that can help you spot an improvable situation. For example: Paul Reeves is an accountant in a business office. One day one of the top brass comes in to talk to Paul's boss, the controller. The executive says, "We need those cost figures by tonight. What can you do?" And the boss says, "It's really an impossible deadline, J.B. Just getting hold of the source data is going to take us about five or six hours."

You've always felt that the procedure for figuring costs had been needlessly complicated because of scattered files and an inefficient filing system. Some day when the pressure is off your boss, you might suggest a reorganization that would make it possible for him to handle requests for cost data more efficiently.

If your relations with your supervisor permit, you may in the course of designated work ask about particular areas that you think represent some kind of problem. And if you ascertain that there are difficulties, you may then get to other things: first, sufficient additional information to get a better idea of the problem and, second, your boss's approval for volunteering to become a one-man task force to try to come up with the solution.

6. *Cooperativeness.* No one can really force you to go along with any kind of "establishment." No one can make you be cooperative on the job unless you really feel that way. But many people mistakenly feel that if they "just do their job" they're earning their pay and therefore being as cooperative as possible. But there is a level of participation that functions above the get-by level. It is exemplified by the employee who observes not only the motions of doing the job but also the spirit.

Henry Turner makes clear his willingness to put his shoulder to the wheel with a single phrase: His supervisor says, "Henry, we're short of the parts you're working on. Would you mind delaying your lunch hour for half an hour so that we can get ahead a little?"

"No problem," says Henry.

The employee for whom going a bit above and beyond the call of duty is "no problem," is the one who usually endears himself to his supervisor. He can be depended on for a little extra effort or for accepting a small temporary inconvenience affably.

It's no mystery that managers in recent years have had their hands full as a result of the don't-give-a-damn, I'll-do-my-job-and-nothing-more attitude. The employee who's willing to put himself out a little will be regarded gratefully as a welcome contrast.

7. *Growth potential.* Every employee has the capacity for growth in his job. In some cases this means improving in present job skills. In others it means acquiring new abilities.

Now it's perfectly clear that no matter how advancement-minded an employee is, there may not be any current opportunity for his promotion.

But growth on the job doesn't necessarily mean moving up the ladder. It could mean becoming a more valuable employee by virtue of increased experience. A particularly desirable kind of experience is the job know-how that people pick up on the job. But there are other roads to this objective: Sarah Rice has been working as a secretary in a large suburban real-estate office. Her job skills are perfectly satisfactory, but she does have aspirations and thinks someday she might want to get a chance to join the firm's sales force. But mainly to add a dimension to her present job as well as to gain some recognition from executives in the firm, she begins studying the local history and land development trends in the area. Pretty soon this knowledge comes up in connection with some of the properties her boss is handling. She can't help but notice that she's made a favorable impression. . . .

An organization is almost human in some ways. It can recognize things that are favorable, view negative developments with disapproval. When a person like Sarah Rice goes out of her way to acquire new information, to conduct herself in a way that's meaningful in company terms, the company can't help but be favorably impressed and its judgment of an employee's worth reflects this evaluation.

5

Getting the Boss on Your Side

THERE is a classic story, recurring in different forms in various media, about the officer in charge of a crowded lifeboat who must decide which passengers to throw over the side so that the rest may survive. The fact is that this situation has arisen in real life in sea disasters throughout the centuries.

Bosses often find themselves in dilemmas similar to that of the lifeboat commander, particularly when times are tough. The stakes are not life or death but rather continuation on the job vs. getting laid off or fired. Of course when there is a massive layoff, the situation is out of the boss's hands; but frequently the manager or supervisor has the final say—or at least considerable influence—on the question of who goes and who stays.

So your boss is a key figure in your campaign to hold on to your job. Bosses, naturally, vary widely in temperament, background, and power, but there are a few basic points on

which we can begin to build techniques for getting the
immediate superior on our side when the crunch comes.

Surprise! He's Human!

Bosses are people. They have the same ranges of like and
dislike, fear and confidence, love and hatred as anyone else.
Most managers dislike firing people. Psychologists point out
that the desire to be admired and loved is one of the most
universal of human traits. Even the "tough" boss wants at
least to be respected, and you do not win respect, let alone
love, by firing people.

Your boss has a personal life independent from his activities on the work scene. He probably worries about
family, money, kids, and the future just as you do. Furthermore he has job problems; none of us is without them.
He would like to make a name for himself, get promoted,
earn a bigger salary. But there are times when ambition is
eclipsed by anxiety about keeping the job. Your boss doesn't
want to be fired any more than you do. If he doesn't
produce, he will lose his job, or his business. (This creates a
need from which you can benefit—as you'll see in the next
chapter.)

It is these pressures, rather than any sadistic personal
preference, that impel the boss to fire people. Sometimes
the order to cut back is passed along to him from his
superiors. More often he feels compelled to anticipate any
such order by cutting back of his own volition. In either
case the boss is apt to be able to exert at least some
discretion in selecting those unfortunates who will receive
the black spot. This of course does not apply to the minority
of situations in which a union agreement imposes a strict
seniority rule on layoffs or firings.

Nevertheless, seniority may well be the controlling
factor—if there are no other factors to offset it. All things

being equal, a boss who is obliged to fire will be tempted to get rid of the most recent employees first. This is not necessarily because he has built up enduring friendships with the veteran members of the work group; often the longer he has worked with a subordinate, the more a boss would like to get rid of him. But resorting to the seniority principle gets the manager off the hook. He can say to himself and to others that he did not play God; he felt that the fair thing to do was to work strictly according to tenure on the job.

However, resorting to seniority may run counter to the boss's need to show good performance in order to keep his own job and enhance his career. He will ignore the seniority rule if he has reason to do so. If you have seniority, you may enjoy an advantage in keeping your job—but don't count on it. There are many thousands of people who thought that length of time in the job gave them protection, only to come to a rude awakening. To cite just one factor in the shakiness of reliance on seniority, we might point out that seniority people are, like as not, making somewhat more money than their juniors for similar work. Furthermore they may have started to coast in their jobs; or they may be giving the impression of coasting, which can be just as bad.

Seniority is fine, but don't figure on it as a guarantee of anything. File it away, and undertake your campaign to win the boss as a job-holding ally just as if you had started a few weeks ago. If you have *not* been around as long as other people, on the other hand, there is no reason to despair. If you play it right, you may even be able to turn your juniority into an advantage.

Sizing Up the Boss
The first step in getting the boss on your side is finding out all you can about him. We are continually astonished by

the number of people who know little or nothing about the individuals for whom they work. To these people the boss is just an order-issuing machine, a depressing but unavoidable element of the job. They never size up the boss in either his business or his personal role.

Getting to know your boss is not just a matter of job survival. It will make you a more effective performer, and it will add interest and diversity to your job. Let's face it; most of us derive satisfactions beyond just a paycheck from the work we do. If we don't enjoy that kind of satisfaction, we wish we did. Would we like it better if we worked for a robot rather than a human being? Though there are times of annoyance when we would voice preference for the robot, by and large we prefer the human being. But if we learn nothing about the human beings for whom we work, we might just as well be reporting to machines.

Your boss has two dimensions—professional and personal. Get to know as much as you can about him in both areas. In terms of his business role, try to find out the answers to such questions as these:

> What is his title?
> How many people report to him?
> Who is *his* boss?
> How long has he been in his present job?
> What is the general opinion of his ability?
> How close is he to moving a step up the ladder?
> Does he communicate better orally or in writing?
> Does he hold many meetings?
> Is he a skillful meeting leader?
> Does he seem to know a lot about the mechanics of the
>   operation he runs?
> Is he on good terms with his colleagues and bosses?
> How much does he make?

And, as to the personal dimension:

> How old is he?
> Is he married? Divorced?
> How many kids? How old are they?
> How is his health? Does he have any chronic problems?
> What kind of a place does he live in?
> How does he spend his leisure time?
> What are his interests and hobbies?
> What does he do for recreation?
> Is he friendly with people whom he knows at work?
> Does he have any personal problems?

The answers to these questions, and others that will suggest themselves to you, should help to flesh out your boss from the abstract being who issues the orders into a flesh-and-blood person. You don't have to conduct the equivalent of an FBI probe to find out about your boss. You needn't raid the personnel files or undertake a cloak-and-dagger surveillance. There's always talk about a manager. Keep your ears open, ask a question now and then, use judgment in separating rumor from fact, and you'll amass a pretty good store of information.

Let the Boss Know You Regard Him as a Person

Everybody's under something of a strain these days at the Zebulon Company. The tightening of the economy has hit this firm as it has hit the entire industry. The word is out that orders have fallen off. The question in the air is, will there be cutbacks?

Nevertheless, business goes on. In the research department people are still getting used to a new boss. Harriet Dampier has been on the job about a month. She is not an ebullient person. Mrs. Dampier is pleasant enough, but reserved. She came into the job with impressive credentials, and—although the research staff has never been enthusiastic about outsiders—they have had to admit that she knows her stuff.

Rita Banks has been in Harriet Dampier's office for half an hour or so, reviewing a project. Mostly it has been a matter of Dampier asking questions—perceptive questions —and Banks trying to come up with the best possible answers. Rita Banks wants to look good. She's been with Zebulon for two years, and feels that she's done a good job, but can she survive a cutback? So she feels it's important to make her answers as informative and to the point as possible.

Finally Dampier says, "Well, Rita, you've given me an excellent fill-in on this job. You seem to have it firmly in hand. Is there anything I can do to help you within the next three weeks before the deadline for presentation of the report?"

Banks says, "No. I can handle it, Mrs. Dampier." On that note the session ends.

Rita Banks is followed by Jane Gehringer, whose visit to Dampier's office is for just about the same purpose—a review of a project that was set in motion before the new department head took up the reins. Dampier and Gehringer go through a similar question-and-answer routine. Dampier says, "I think I've found out what I need to know about this job, Jane. Is there anything I can tell you or do for you as you wrap it up?"

Unlike her colleague Rita, who left the boss's office quickly, Jane Gehringer lingers a moment. "Well," she says, "I have filled you in on this as best I can, and I think I see what needs to be done from here in. But I was wondering—you may have some different ideas about writing it up. I can follow the procedure we've always used, and if that's OK with you, fine. But it occurred to me that you might have some better ideas about presentation."

Dampier thinks about this for a moment. Then: "As a matter of fact, there might be one or two points where I'd consider a departure from the format you're used to. What would you think of this, Jane?" The manager outlines a few changes that might be made. Gehringer discusses them, suggests a modification or two, and they come to agreement. As she is gathering up her papers, Gehringer says, "Oh—this is out of the business area, Mrs. Dampier, but I heard something about your little boy—Rick is his name, isn't it?—breaking his wrist. I hope it isn't anything too serious."

Dampier looks a little surprised. Then she smiles. "Why, no, it's a clean break and he's mending nicely. He's back in school and very proud of his cast, getting everyone in sight to autograph it. He fell out of a tree, you know. There is no way to keep them from climbing. I know that you haven't got any children, so you have yet to experience the joy and agony of watching them grow up."

Jane Gehringer laughs, "It's something to look forward to, I guess. Well, please give Rick my best and tell him to quit playing Tarzan for a while." Dampier smiles again in response: "I'll tell him, although a fat lot of good it will do. Thank you for the thought."

The business content of these two conversations was, for all practical purposes, identical. Both Banks and Gehringer know their jobs; each was able to report competently and succinctly. But Jane Gehringer added a couple of extras. For one thing she gave the boss a chance to express some ideas and to make some suggestions. Some people—particularly with a new boss—seem tightly on guard against presenting an opening for the boss to offer comments. They have a possessive feeling about the job and think that they know better than the boss how to handle the nuts and bolts. (This may be true, but in terms of superior-subordinate relations it is somewhat irrelevant.) Or they have become "grooved" in their way of doing things and wish to forestall for as long as possible any change that might make things more difficult. But mostly this tendency to clam up in conversation with the boss stems from an attitude that characterizes the boss as a necessary annoyance at best, an enemy at worst, always a source of worry but never a living, breathing human being.

Within a few minutes Jane Gehringer accomplished two things. She acknowledged the new manager's natural desire to begin to make some changes in things. Some bosses are diffident about changing things when they arrive on the job; others plunge right in. Harriet Dampier is one of those bosses who proceeds cautiously. Gehringer gave her the chance to express some opinions without making it seem as if the new boss were being critical or insisting on having her own way.

And—Jane Gehringer indicated that she thought of the boss as a person, with worries, problems, a family to take care of. Rita Banks had heard about young Rick Dampier's accident, but it did not occur to her to say anything about it. After all, it had nothing to do with business. Well, if business were conducted among androids there would, of course, be no room for this kind of trivial human exchange. But since bosses share the human state with us, they are likely to respond to an occasional recognition of the fact that life is lubricated by sympathetic and cordial exchanges between those who live it.

Is it apple polishing to let the boss know that you are aware of him as a human being? Rita Banks might consider it to be so. She would probably be scornful of Jane Gehringer, proclaiming that Gehringer was just buttering up the manager so that she could be surer of hanging on to her job.

Let's look at the question squarely. Suppose this sort of

thing—letting the boss know you see him as an individual—*is* nothing but what is commonly called apple polishing, or—even more commonly—kissing ass. The authors of this book are concerned with helping people to keep their jobs. We make few, if any, value judgments. Oh, we might hesitate to suggest that a jobholder enter into slavery or prostitution or sign away an immortal soul to hang on to a paycheck. But we are somewhat more than skeptical about the conventional wisdom that decrees it to be self-abasement to have a good word to say to—or about—the boss.

However, the question here does not revolve around such considerations. Gehringer was not just buttering up the boss. She was helping to establish a relationship between two people who have to work with each other. The fact that they are boss and subordinate does not make it any less important that a good relationship be established. If anything, it is even more important. If we want the boss to consider us as human beings, with problems and needs that are peculiarly our own, it is only reasonable that we extend the same kind of recognition in the other direction.

Naturally this can be overdone. Take the case of Dave Moore. Busy at his job, Moore sees his boss, Lee Petroni, approaching. Moore stops working, wipes his hands, and exclaims, "How's the boy, Lee? Did they get that transmission straightened out for you? I'm telling you, getting a decent mechanic these days is like finding gold. I had the same problem with my Matador, you know, and what I finally had to do . . ." There follows a long description of Moore's trials and tribulations in the automotive area, which branches into a couple of fairly funny jokes and an insistent suggestion that the Petronis join the Moores for an evening of bowling on the forthcoming Saturday night.

Lee Petroni takes as much of this as he can, as patiently as he can. Finally he manages to break in with an urgent question about the job. Moore answers casually, then resumes the personal conversation. Petroni interrupts rather brusquely and walks away. Moore looks after him, thinking, "Some guys become bosses and right away they haven't got any time for us peons. He's got a big head."

Insistent and exaggerated insertion of a personal note into an exchange with the boss does not facilitate the relationship. But when you can—naturally and gracefully—let the boss know that you are aware of his humanity, you have started to develop a healthy avenue of exchange, and you are giving yourself a better chance to assure retention of the job.

In short, what we recommend are moves aimed at building a healthy, friendly relationship between you and your boss, one that will make you stand out in his mind in a favorable way—and stack the cards in your favor when the chips are down. Here's a brief wrap-up:

Do's and Don'ts of Personal Contacts

Do go about your friendship-building moves naturally—at appropriate times and places.

Don't force matters, or overdo the personal exchange. Be ready to ease off if the boss seems disinterested.

Don't pry. In the attempt to forge a good relationship, don't move into personal areas that he may think are off limits for business friends.

Do put business before pleasure. There should be a balance between business and personal contacts—and business, as traditional wisdom properly has it, should have precedence.

Do try to make it an even exchange between you. Be as open with the boss as he or she is with you—not much more or much less.

Don't let your friendly relations embarrass him. Avoid

trading on your good standing with him, or ex-
pecting him to show favoritism. You're saving
that—if necessary—for the key situation: if and
when the job turns shaky.

Ask for the Boss's Help

Most of us try to develop our skills on the job, and, when we
develop them, we are proud of our accomplishments. We
hope that others, notably those to whom we report, will
recognize our abilities. But even if recognition is slow in
coming, we take pleasure in our capabilities.

The natural corollary to this is that we develop self-
sufficiency to the point at which we don't have to ask
anyone for help in performing the job; or, even if we could
use some help, we are reluctant to ask for it. Steve Plummer
is a man who has developed skills at his job of which he is
quite proud. He shies away from requesting advice or
assistance. So why, as we look in on Steve, is he asking his
boss, Rod Green, for some assistance?

That's what Steve Plummer is doing: "Rod, whenever I
get one of these calls asking about a delivery date, I follow a
certain routine. I ask questions to get all the particulars.
Then I telex the factory and get feedback on the job. Then I
call the customer back with the information. But sometimes
it takes a while for the factory to feed back. You know how
it is, they don't know where all the jobs are at any given
time. What I'm wondering is, with times and competition
so tough, would it be worthwhile to make some changes in
this procedure with certain customers? For instance, we
might assign some customers for special handling. Then, if
it's taking more than six hours to get the dope from the
plant, make an interim call to the customer to give him
some feeling that we're working on it, but mostly to sort of

hold his hand. It would take some time and a little expense, but it seems to me that there might be a point to it in terms of customer relations."

Now, there are several ways that Steve Plummer might have handled this idea. He has enough autonomy in his job to be able to modify his procedure, without asking anybody about it. Or, he might state his idea in terms of a positive suggestion.

Instead, Plummer is asking Green for advice. He is doing this for a well-thought-out reason; he wants to develop a more solid relationship with the boss so that he has a better chance of keeping his job when others lose theirs.

There are a few bosses who don't want to be asked for help at any time. But very few, and they don't last long. Most bosses *want* to get into the act. Some managers are frustrated training directors. They itch to plunge in there and help out their subordinates.

But often the subordinate does not give the boss an opening. Armed with his own pride, confidence and self-sufficiency, he makes it clear that he wants to be left alone to do his thing. If the boss horns in to make some suggestions, the subordinate listens; but he listens with a kind of controlled patience that makes it clear that the boss is an intruder. So the boss does not get a chance to train or help as many people as he'd like.

When you ask the boss for help you are, of course, opening up an avenue toward improvement of your job skills. Chances are that the boss knows something that can help you. But here we are concerned with job security. The employee who enlists his boss's assistance may be taking a long stride in the direction of job security for two reasons. First, he is affording the boss a chance to do some training and to shape a subordinate in the direction he wants. Second, he is setting in motion forces that will get the boss to make an investment of time and effort in this particular worker, namely, you.

When a manager has taken the trouble to do some development work with a subordinate, he begins to feel an interest in that person's progress. After all, the worker's subsequent success will serve as testimony to the boss's soundness of judgment and ability to train. The boss will be reluctant to throw away such an investment before it has had a chance to come to maturity.

So it might be a good idea to consider asking your boss for some special help in the way of advice or training. Be ready to accept the help, pay attention to the advice, and show some progress in picking up the tips he imparts to you. If you demonstrate enough responsiveness and results to satisfy him, your continued development will become a project of more than passing interest to him. And, when things get tight, he is apt to look favorably on the option of keeping you around. Firing you would almost amount to an admission of failure on his part.

6

Helping the Boss Help You

The previous chapter explains the key importance of your boss in your job situation, and suggests a number of moves you can make to get him to see you in a favorable light.

There is a further step you can take in this possibly crucial relationship: You can *strengthen his hand*, and by reinforcing his position and clout, you gain a stronger ally.

Start of the process is the effort to emphasize your individuality. You want him to be very much aware of your presence, and the capabilities you have that can be helpful to him.

Get the Boss to Think of You as an Individual

The administrative department of Cavalier Enterprises has been struggling for a week with the logistics of an office-wide reorganization. Divisions are being shifted around wholesale; the phones are abuzz with the requests and complaints of people who are unhappy with the way the change is going. Everybody in administration is knocking himself out to cope with the crisis.

Office manager Gene Freed is hustling right along with all of his employees. He moves from desk to desk, straightening out problems, trying to keep chins up. One of his recurring comments is, "Well, these things do come up. It's not so bad, is it?" In response to this most people grit their teeth and agree: "No, Gene, it's not so bad. We'll get through it." Whether they feel this way or not, they have the impression that this is the answer that Gene Freed wants to hear. Certainly it seems to be the answer he expects to hear. At any rate, it's what he's getting.

It's what he's getting, that is, until he talks to Mitch Latham. Latham offers a somewhat different response: "Not so bad? It's terrible! Nobody outside this department seems to understand what we're up against here. Don't get me wrong, Gene. I'm doing my damnedest just like you and everybody else, but when we get this thing licked we've got to figure out some way to keep from getting in a spot like this again. I'm picking up a few ideas about that as I go along, and I hope everybody else is as well."

In the hours and days that follow, Gene Freed keeps a particular eye on Mitch Latham. That's a natural reaction on the boss's part. He will take note of the individual who does not seem to react as the others do, especially in a crisis. Of course, at first, Freed wonders if he's got a problem with Latham. He asks himself if this worker is malingering or expressing the kind of disaffection that will spread to the rest of the group. But no. Latham turns out to be working just as hard as his colleagues, and maybe harder. And there's no reason to think that Mitch Latham is griping inordinately to his fellow workers. He confines his expressions of anger and concern to the boss.

During a coffee break Freed makes it a point to talk with

Latham again. Latham repeats his feelings that the department shouldn't get into this kind of situation again. He refers to the fact that his wife, Angie, and their two children, Chris and Melinda, have hardly seen him for the past three weeks. Latham drops other personal and professional notes into the conversation, and winds up reiterating his determination to come up with some thoughts that will forestall a repetition of the emergency. Gene Freed doesn't necessarily buy it all, but he listens to what Latham has to say.

By means of this "different" behavior Mitch Latham has accomplished something important. He has gotten the boss to think of him as an *individual*, not as just another one of the people in the department.

Of course there are ways and ways of getting the boss to see you as an individual. If Latham had simply bitched excessively about the work load, and fulminated in the presence of the others on the job, he would have been carving out an equally individual image for himself, but a distinctly unfavorable one. The idea is to get the boss to think of you as being different in a positive, not a negative, sense.

If Latham had confined his remarks to the family disruptions caused by the spate of overtime work, he would not have been nearly as effective. After all, everybody, including Freed, was working long hours. But Mitch Latham established his point of difference by making some potentially constructive observations about the job. Having done this his additional remarks about his personal existence contributed to the boss's picture of him as an individual.

This is not to suggest that Mitch Latham did and said these things as part of a carefully thought-out plan, calculating every word in advance. He probably did no such thing. The point, however, is this: When you determine to establish yourself as an individual with the boss, you can—to some degree—shape your spontaneous remarks in ways that will bring you the small amount of positive attention that will come in handy later. You've built the bridge. Now you can come across.

Your Role as the Boss's Sounding Board

Bosses tend to lose touch with what is going on within their operations. This is an inevitable side effect of promotion to greater responsibility. Commentators on supervision and management have spoken and written extensively about this phenomenon. It has a considerable influence on the concept that has come to be known as the "Peter Principle"—the idea that people are ultimately promoted to their "levels of incompetence." An individual doesn't become incompetent when he gets a bigger job; but his increasing remoteness from day-to-day operations contributes to the lack of reliability in his decisions, and the result is the appearance of incompetence.

Bosses need to be able to talk with somebody. They can talk with other bosses, but such conversations tend to deal in abstractions rather than the nitty-gritty of running the operation. Many managers feel a distinct need to chat about work with subordinates, but this entails problems, not the least of which is the attitude of many subordinates.

It is not unnatural for workers to look upon the boss with derision and, sometimes, enmity. These feelings may grow out of envy, but they are no less strong for that. Here is a typical exchange between two salesmen who are talking about their boss, the regional sales manager. One says, "Would you believe that Sam said to me the other day that he wanted to 'kick around' some ideas about reorganizing the territories? 'Kick around,' that's what he said. So I said,

'What do you have in mind, Sam?' When I heard what he was thinking I could hardly keep from laughing. I'm telling you, he hasn't got a clue about the way we cover territories out here these days."

The other salesman responds, "When you've been around as long as I have, you'll get the picture. All managers are alike. They sit there and push papers around, but they couldn't sell beer to the Elks. I guess Sam wasn't a bad salesman when he was out carrying a case, but he doesn't have it anymore."

It's human to poke fun at the man who stands a rung above us on the ladder. There is something in all of us that responds to the sight of the guy in the high hat slipping on a banana peel. When we find that the boss seems to know less than we do about details of the job, we tend to cherish that discovery as a kind of consolation for our own relative lack of recognition.

We can be sure that Sam, the sales manager referred to in the conversation between these two salesmen, will not soon repeat his effort to talk things over—at least not with this particular representative. But that does not diminish his need to talk with somebody.

Let's look at an example of how this fact of life can be turned to practical benefit. Linda Bruce knows that her boss, Ed Halloran, is concerned about the chaotic state of the files in the department. Halloran has issued several sets of instructions designed to lead to improvement, but nothing seems to work. Bruce's colleagues appear to derive gleeful satisfaction from Halloran's frustration. They have to cope with the inefficient system, it is true; but the general attitude seems to be that they get paid anyway, and the shortcomings of the operation are the boss's problem.

One day Linda Bruce is seated next to Halloran's desk, receiving instructions on a job. That morning there has been another in the recurring episodes of confusion due to inadequate filing organization. Bruce has more or less shared the general attitude that Halloran's futile flailings are kind of funny, but he looks so woebegone and distracted that she is impelled to say something. She has nothing constructive to suggest, so all she can say is, "I know how much you'd like to get the filing straightened out. It is a mess."

Halloran cocks an inquiring eye at her. Then he says, "Yeah, that it is. Nobody's fault, really; we just inherited years of neglect, and the system isn't up to the demands we're making on it. I've tried a few things, but they didn't get very far. I don't have to tell you that, Linda. But I keep thinking there must be some simple thing that I'm overlooking. Everybody says that the way to do it is to get more space, but I'm beginning to wonder. Seems to me that we couldn't lose anything by thinking about a different approach. . . ."

The boss proceeds to talk about a number of possible avenues of attack on the problem. Linda Bruce does little more than listen and make appropriate responses. At the end of their talk Halloran thanks her for the discussion, and he sounds as if he really means it. Within the next few weeks, he speaks to her several more times in much the same way.

Linda Bruce is actively *doing* next to nothing. Her role is that of a listener. Nevertheless she is accomplishing two things. She is performing a service for the boss and the department, and she is enhancing her own job-keeping potential.

Even if you contribute little to the exchange, you can serve as a useful sounding board for the boss. You do this by listening and reacting. The boss is able to try out ideas as he carries on a monologue. In truth he may be talking to himself. Nevertheless you are there as the ostensible listener. Furthermore he is able to gauge your reaction to various notions by observing your expression and your gestures—or the absence of them. Once the boss gets used to you as a dependable sounding board, he will come to rely on your presence in this capacity. This does not convert you into a ball of fire as far as the job is concerned, but it helps you in various ways. You learn something about your boss, your company, and your job. You help your boss to be more creative by giving him an opportunity to bounce ideas off of you. And you begin to carve out that slight edge that can make all the difference.

There is a possible side effect. Certain co-workers will wonder about all the time you are spending listening to the boss. There may be remarks about it. But you don't have to describe the role you're playing. If you say little in a judicious way, people may even think that the boss is spending all that time chewing you out. But even if they do catch on to the fact that you are acting as sounding board for the brass, you can shrug off their comments as you remind yourself that you are not only solidifying your hold on your job but performing a service to the entire operation.

Conveying Information

The role of sounding board is passive. You can strengthen your relationship with the boss by becoming a more active contributor to the exchange. To do this you need not take a short course at the Harvard Graduate School of Business Administration. All you have to do is talk about your job and the things you observe while doing the job.

Randy Schultz is having a cup of coffee with his boss, Jess Osaka. This is not a premeditated appointment. Osaka happened to be talking with Schultz when coffee-break time rolled around. They had been talking about results. Osaka was asking if it would be possible to make some adjustments so that a certain run of units could be produced with a new feature. Schultz replied that it could be done, after repositioning the machine tools in shaping the unit.

Now, in a relaxed moment, Schultz starts to talk about *how* the job is to be done and some of the peculiarities of the machinery. "You know," he says, "there's a trick to it. Ordinarily you would have to figure on a few hours' downtime to make a new setup for that kind of change, but there are things you can do in positioning the blanks that will speed it up. If you're interested, I can show you. . . ."

Osaka, being a savvy boss, is interested. He knows full well that the guy who is actually doing the job picks up shortcuts that don't necessarily get back to the boss. The fact that a supervisor or manager used to perform the same operation himself does not matter. If he's been away from it for a while, technology and technique have changed enough so that he is out of touch.

As Schultz explains the shortcut, he is performing a valuable service to the boss. It is not that Osaka figures that he is going to be running the equipment himself. The importance, rather, lies in the additional "feel" for the job that Schultz is helping Osaka to acquire. The next time the boss is trying to figure out how to gauge the time necessary for a special run, he will be able to crank some new facts into his deliberations.

You can be a source of information for the boss about the details of the work you are involved in, its special problems, the things he should look for. Most bosses welcome this kind of data. It enables them to better understand what's going on, and to talk the proper language and ask the right questions in working with subordinates.

But this is not the only way in which you can convey

information. You can fill the boss in on other matters that are important to him. Here's an example: Ken Fodor doesn't perform work that involves any special inside dope, but he is able to be useful as a resource nevertheless. Right now, for example, he is reflecting to his supervisor his feelings about a recent change in the organization: "I couldn't say I speak for any of the other guys, but the way I see it, the new setup is kind of a pain now, but I'll be used to it before long. I liked being able to walk over to the toolroom and getting whatever I wanted, and I can't do that anymore. But the new procedure is not a big deal, and I realize the basic idea behind it is to make sure we can get the things we need without wasting any time looking all over the place for the person who's got them."

The boss listens with some care. While Fodor states that he is speaking only for himself, the boss has gotten to feel that this particular subordinate does reflect general feelings among the work group, and thus his comments are valuable. It is frequently not too easy for a boss to pick up this kind of feel accurately; to the extent that you can help him to get it, you are making yourself more valuable to him. And also of notable importance, you're making him more valuable to *himself*.

Let's be clear: The sort of information we are describing is neither gripe nor gossip. The boss does not welcome hearing about the details of a subordinate's job when they are conveyed in terms of complaint: "When the whole department is busy at the keyboards you can't hear yourself think. It's driving us all crazy." And while he might welcome gossip ("They say Jim's wife threw him out of the house last night"), it is dangerous to become a dealer in it unless you are absolutely sure of what you're doing. You are apt to become highly unpopular among your colleagues; so much so that, in a pinch, you are a liability and your chances of being cut from the squad are increased rather than diminished. Also the boss who may welcome the latest rumors from you is likely to do so with the mental note that you are probably dishing up the dirt about him as well.

However, with these reservations in mind, you should consider yourself as a potential source of useful information for the boss, and make use of that fact to build the relationship.

Now, as the final step in helping the boss help you, of giving his capabilities a shot in the arm that eventually can benefit you, consider the advantages when you:

Become an In-House Consultant

The most secure worker is the one whose boss's job security is tied in closely with his own. There are times when you can build your value considerably as a job-keeping resource for the person to whom you report.

Of course part of this is a function of your everyday conduct as regards the boss. Speak well of him. Support him rather than undercut him. Do your job in a way that makes him look good.

But there may be even more that you can do. The spot to aim for is that of the unofficial in-house consultant to the boss.

We live in an age of consultants. Experts command large sums for handing out advice. But this does not mean that they possess an unlimited store of magic answers and solutions to problems. Peter Drucker, the dean of business consultants, remarked to us: "I don't want to have people leave my office saying, 'I never knew that before.' Rather they should be saying, 'I knew that, but I wasn't using it.' " You can work with your boss to make him more effective in his job—and that is the essence of consultation.

Here's how Jay Drum does it. He's chatting with his boss,

Herman Kriegel, about several problems that have been assailing the operation. They have covered a lot of details; now they are talking in more general terms. Drum puts a question: "Herman, we have a number of things to think about here. If we could, by concentrating on it, come up with a good answer to just one of these problems by the end of next week, which one would you want solved first?"

Kriegel thinks about this and they discuss it. A little while later Drum has another question: "If we had unlimited resources, what's the most effective way that you can see to solve that problem the quickest?" After some thought Kriegel comes up with the answer. This is greeted by another question from Drum: "How would you trim that solution down to fit into the setup we have here now?" Both Kriegel and Drum contribute to answering that one.

Jay Drum is not doing Herman Kriegel's thinking for him. He is helping the boss to think more clearly. He is doing this by asking the kinds of questions that lead toward establishment of priorities, focusing on a single problem rather than a multitude of issues, and development of a working hypothesis that leads toward a solution. The boss has no reason to feel that Drum is trying to insinuate himself into matters of policy. The subordinate is just using his knowledge of the boss and the operation to ask questions that require some thinking and that lead toward progress in solving problems.

This is the proper way to establish yourself as an in-house consultant. (The wrong way is to breeze in and say "Herman, if I were in your shoes, here's how I'd clean up this mess.") And, to solidify your unofficial consulting role, you can bring to bear your own viewpoint on things, which should serve as a useful aid in getting the boss to see things more clearly. For example, you may find yourself playing "devil's advocate," testing his tentative solutions with tough questions: "Just for the sake of argument, suppose we had a strike and the supply of raw material was cut off for as much as a month. Would this answer still hold up?"

Let's be very clear that the role of the in-house consultant is *not* that of a yes-man. Without doubt there are still bosses who can be beguiled by assiduous and uncritical agreement with everything they say. But, even while a manager may get a kind of pleasure from this sort of flattery, he is likely to be somewhat contemptuous of the source. In a pinch the yes-man may well have far less support in the boss's office then he expected. The boss may even feel obliged to bend over backward in being tough on the yes-man, to prove to himself and others that he is not affected by boot licking.

If you know your job, and have some feel for overall organizational problems, you can work toward the establishment of an in-house consulting relationship that can be a pillar of strength in underpinning the security of your job.

We have covered some of the more important and accessible ways in which you can get the boss on your side. There are, of course, variations of these, and others that we have not space to cover. All of these suggestions are *job-oriented;* they have nothing to do with the development of extra-friendly relationships with the boss. If you can become his buddy, that's swell; but it's something that happens or does not happen. We don't suggest pure friendship as a job-keeping ploy.

The essence of this approach to winning the boss's support as job-insurance lies in these steps; covered in both this and the previous chapter:

- Understand your boss, his job and his problems;
- Get to know the boss as a person;
- Let him know that you see him as a person;

- Enlist the boss's help in developing your skills;
- Give him a chance to know you as an individual;
- Serve as a sounding board for the boss's ideas;
- Become a source of useful information;
- Serve as an in-house consultant.

None of these steps require any special training or skill. They do require that your attitude toward the boss be one that acknowledges his fellow humanity and involves some sympathy for his need to perform well and strengthen his grip on his own job. You can't continue to regard the boss as an adversary or a lackey of the establishment or a lucky buffoon. But once you have examined your own feelings and generated a positive attitude toward the individual to whom you report, you are ready to build a campaign that will enlist him as an ally.

There is one other point that should be made about this plan. Everything that we suggest here is designed to make you a more rewarding person to know, in terms of human relationships as well as your ability to do a good job. And who knows? If your boss-cultivating project leads to improvement in yourself, the boss and the organization, there may never be any reason to be concerned about losing your job.

7

The Politics of Job Strengthening

THE average company is, in many ways, a political institution. There are no parties in the formal sense, but there are splits over issues and informal party groupings. There are no official elections—but there are certainly winners and losers. There are campaigns, maneuvers for advantage, and propaganda programs. And there are certain other aspects of the governmental political scene: arm twisting, treachery, and dirty tricks.

Your company may not have such long-established party organizations as the Democrats and Republicans, but there are parties nevertheless. These intra-company parties form around issues or around individuals. Some of them, though never officially recognized, are of great influence and long standing. You can—and this is highly pertinent to the problem of holding on to your job—become enrolled in one of your company's parties without even knowing about it.

73

Liberals and Conservatives at Elysian

Elysian, Inc., is a small-to-medium manufacturing firm. Over the years there has developed a distinct split in the executive committee of Elysian. Some members of top management are all for a go-go policy of expansion. They want to get into new, "hot" consumer lines and, as they put it, "bring Elysian into the twentieth century." In effect these people constitute the "Liberal" party.

They are opposed by the "Conservatives." The Conservatives have always maintained that Elysian is OK the way it is now and has always been. They insist on sticking to the small line of products and restricted distribution channels that the company knows best. They say that to go running off after the illusion of mushroom growth is too risky and that it's better to keep plugging away in the traditional avenues.

For most of the time the Conservatives have held the upper hand at Elysian. Once, ten years ago, the Liberals managed to amass enough power to influence the top brass to make some startling innovations. Startling, at least for Elysian. But the chief executive officer of the company, old Si McDermott, never really liked the changes, and when he reestablished a greater measure of power in the executive committee, the new departures were quietly laid to rest, and several "Young Turks" departed the scene.

Si McDermott is the boss, but he does not rule with unrestricted power. The members of the executive committee represent the principal ownership interests in Elysian, and McDermott has been able to maintain a balance in favor of his conservative policies. The Liberals are still around. Indeed, with their drive and talent, they are necessary to the company, and nobody knows that better than Si McDermott—but they are, as they usually have been, the "outs."

Being Out of Politics May Mean Being in Trouble

Now we come to Larry Keene. Larry has not been with Elysian for very long. He is not at the policy-making level. Larry Keene is a bright, energetic young fellow, with a good background and track record, who was hired because he showed promise and because there was a specific lower-management job for him to fill.

Keene rarely enters the inner sanctum. He is not consulted on matters of overall policy, except when one of the brass hats wants some specific input. Larry does his day-to-day job, does it well, and enjoys it. So what's his problem?

Larry Keene doesn't know it yet, but *he is in trouble.* Above the clouds at Elysian, a new act in the long struggle is about to begin. Vice-President Will Trask, the current leader of the Liberal faction, has massed his forces carefully. He has swung some of the less dedicated Conservatives around to his way of thinking. Trask is ready to make a new and potent bid for power. Maybe he will not depose Si McDermott, at least not right away, but he aims to diminish McDermott's scope and to move Elysian along some new directions. This will involve certain organizational changes as well as some new policies.

Why should this affect Larry Keene? After all Larry is not a member in good standing of either the Liberal or the Conservative party. He is only remotely aware that the split exists. He does what he is told and does it loyally and with dispatch. Will Trask knows who Larry Keene is, and what he does, but Trask has no reason to bear any grudges against the younger man.

But it's not a matter of personalities. There is a law of corporate life that dictates that new brooms tend to sweep as clean as they can. When Trask achieves greater power, he is going to make some changes. And one of those changes is likely to be Larry Keene. Larry, while not a policy-

making Conservative, has acquired a patina of Conservative coloration. He was, after all, brought in by the
ruling party. So McDermott and some of the other leading
Conservatives like him, and have been free to say so. And
so, without knowing it, Larry Keene has been enrolled in
one of the contending parties. When that party loses a
measure of power, his head goes on the block. Will Trask
will not be able to get rid of Si McDermott and his senior
colleagues, but he is going to have enough clout to get rid of
Larry Keene, redesign Larry's job, and bring in somebody
who may not be better, but who will be Trask's man. This
may not be very fair, and it is certainly unfortunate for
Larry Keene, but it is the way things happen.

The internecine political struggle that menaces an un-
suspecting worker need not be of long-standing, nor need it
concern a fundamental disagreement over high-level
policy. It may be short-lived and almost purely personal—but none the less lethal to the victim.

How Favoritism Grows—Or Is Gained

Take the case of Marge Glossop. Glossop has worked in the
accounting department at the Grunion Company for five
years. When she joined the department she was befriended
by Edna Allessio, one of the veterans of the organization.
Allessio taught Glossop the ropes, held her hand when
things were tough, and served as her mentor and guide.

Although Marge Glossop had no such thought in mind,
having a friend like Edna Allessio was a pretty good deal.
Allessio worked closely with Lu Gear, the department
head. Gear listened to Allessio and sought her advice on
things. In many ways Edna Allessio was the unofficial
runner of accounting, at least in many of its workaday
aspects.

But within the past year a new factor has entered the

picture. Gerry Clatworthy hasn't been around as long as Allessio, but she has shown she knows her stuff. Gerry resents Allessio's ascendance and would like to have more say in the way things are done there. She has been talking to Lu Gear, saying, "Lu, you really ought to be more independent and forceful in putting your ideas across. You have some great ideas; but they often get lost in the shuffle because you have been trying to filter them through certain parties who just don't like new ideas." And so on.

This is getting to Lu Gear. Gear is beginning to "think more independently"—which means, in reality, relying more on Clatworthy than on Allessio. And all of this could not have come about at a worse time for Marge Glossop. There is a reorganization coming; some jobs will be eliminated and some people will depart. If Gear were still working primarily with Allessio as a confidante, Marge Glossop would not have to worry. But Clatworthy will now have a lot to say about what happens—and Marge is definitely not one of Gerry Clatworthy's girls. It's got nothing to do with ability; Clatworthy simply happens to have her own favorites. So Marge Glossop—whether she realizes it or not—is in great danger of losing her job.

Check Your Own Political Situation

What's the political situation in your company and your work group—and how do you stand in it? Here are some questions to ask yourself.

The Company

> Are there identifiable cliques in the top echelons?
> How long have they existed?
> Is one clique usually dominant? Or do they shift?
> What's the nature of the difference? Policy? Personality? A combination?

How much emphasis is put on new employees "fitting in?"

Who are the leaders of the cliques?

Do they tend to turn against those who are not "with them?"

Is there a power struggle going on now?

Can you identify someone near the top who may be getting ready to try for dominance?

Can you describe that individual's "political" preferences?

Which members of upper management do you know best?

Do they all tend to fall into a similar political pattern?

Are you identified with any particular sect or club within the company?

When people are laid off, what is the basis? Seniority? Ability? Whom they know?

How long has the present dominant faction (or individual) been in power?

The Work Group

Is your immediate boss politically "in" or "out?"

Does he play favorites and have particular friends in the department?

How do you stand with the boss? Do you like him? Does he like you?

Are there distinct cliques in your work group?

What is the basis on which cliques form? Age? Seniority? Social preferences?

How much influence does politics have on the work? Do favorites get better assignments and evaluations?

Which people are closest to your immediate boss? How do you stand with them?

Has anyone ever referred—jokingly or otherwise—to your standing with the boss?

Which clique do you think an outsider might identify you with?

Which clique would you prefer to be part of?

Do you think a change in leadership is coming?

How do you think you might stand if there is a change?

You

Do you like to "play politics"?

Do you make a deliberate effort to stay out of company politics?

Do you say much about your opinions as to how things are done?

In general, are you a supporter or an opponent of the boss?

Which individuals are least friendly toward you? Which most friendly?

How influential are your friends? Your enemies?

Do you have many friends on the job?

Do your friends tend to fall into a pattern, or are they all different?

Have you ever asked for a favor based on friendship?

Has anybody ever complained about you to the boss?

Do your colleagues trust you? Who doesn't? Why not?

How often do you have a relaxed talk with the boss? With other influential members of the group?

What Should You Do?

A careful review of the situation will give you a better idea of the political ecology of your company and your work group, and where you stand. The next question is, what can you do about it?

You can't ignore it. Distasteful as the thought may be, politics might have a lot to do with your chances of keeping your job. Unfortunately this is true even if you detest company politics and try to stay out of it. You can ignore it if you prefer—but your ignoring it does not make it any less potent. The ostrich with his head in the sand will not slow down the approach of the lion simply by refusing to look at it.

The recognition that there is such a thing as politics is the first step. Your subsequent moves will depend on the situation and on your personal position and proclivities. The following are some tips on various ways of maneuvering, drawn from the experience of veteran company politicians.

How About Enlightened Fence Sitting?

You will often hear it said that "you can't just sit on the fence." Why can't you? True, there is something in the American tradition that induces us to look askance at the fence sitter. We prefer the individual who takes a definite stand, who climbs down off the fence into the arena on one side or the other.

But let's not write off fence sitting too quickly. Your best bet in a political situation may be to try to maintain reasonable relationships with *both* sides. But this is not merely a passive exercise, involving only sitting there and averting your eyes from what is going on. On the contrary, remaining alive in the middle takes flexibility and resourcefulness.

If—so far as you are able to determine—you are not thoroughly identified with a particular side or clique, learn as much as you can about the influential political forces that surround you. Go through the questions listed above and work to come up with hard answers. Don't click off your consciousness when people talk about the boss, or the company, or the department. Avoid committing yourself, but do plenty of hard listening.

Keeping a position between contending camps requires you to offer a certain amount of evidence to both sides of your sympathy and understanding, if not your full agreement and total enlistment. But this is not simply a matter of talking with X at three o'clock and saying, "By God, X, I couldn't agree with you more"; and then turning around at four o'clock to vow to Y, "I am one hundred percent on your side." This is not fence sitting; it is an attempt to get down on both sides of the fence at the same time. You can't be comfortable while doing it; it will split, at the very least, your personality. And it isn't worth trying, because it is impossible and will ultimately lead to alienation of both sides.

Instead make an effort to understand what the people on each side are saying. Listen to them; evaluate the points. Then do your best to find some point on which you can agree with the contending positions.

For example, the division that Walter Klemm works in is split over the boss, Terry Walkinshaw. To some degree it is a matter of Walkinshaw's personality—and in all candor Klemm has to admit to himself that he would never vote for the boss in a world-wide popularity contest. But it's more than personality. Walkinshaw has installed some new work regulations that have not exactly met with acclaim.

Ned Yeager—leader of the anti-Walkinshaw forces and a potential successor—is active and articulate in stimulating discontent. Here he is, doing his number with Klemm: "Walter, the problem is not that Terry is a bastard, but he is such a stupid bastard. I saw all those forms you had to fill out to get a special shipment of envelopes. You can't tell me that this did not screw up your operation, at least for the day. Really, it's too much, don't you think?"

Klemm replies, "Yeah. The paperwork burns me up

sometimes. I think the requirement is stupid, all right, but that doesn't necessarily make Terry stupid for putting it in. Maybe they made him do it. Maybe he has something in mind that we don't know about. I agree that I can't see what it is, but maybe we ought to ask him."

Yeager responds scornfully, "If he had a good reason for doing it, don't you think he would have let us know? It's just a lot of extra Mickey Mouse work that he thinks will impress the guys at the top. If we can make it clear that it's really lousing up the operation, then we'll all be better off. You know, the overall performance of this department has not been all that great lately. That should worry every one of us. It sure bothers me."

Klemm shrugs. "It bothers me, too. But I can't just ignore the possibility that Terry may have some good reasons in mind but is just not able to explain them to us." Yeager starts to say something, but Klemm forestalls him: "He *should* be able to explain it, that's his job, but we know that there is a personality problem here as well. Terry doesn't come across that well, and he knows some of us don't like him. I guess we can't help the personalities we are born with, and he sure didn't get the best of the deal when they were handing them out. But it seems to me that has to put a damper on things when he tries to communicate."

Not long afterward Klemm is talking with the boss. Walkinshaw says, "I got your requisitions. At least you fill the damn things out. Some of these zombies don't understand simple English. It's not that much of a problem to do them, is it?"

Klemm says, "Terry, I have to tell you that it *is* a problem. But solving problems and doing what we are supposed to do is what we get paid for. I'm not going to kid you—I wish I didn't have to do all that paperwork. But I go on the assumption that you have a good reason for it. But the reason is not clear to a lot of the guys."

Walkinshaw curtly gives Klemm an explanation for the procedure. It is far from adequate, but Klemm figures it's the best he is going to get. Afterward, talking with Yeager, he says "If you're interested, here's what Terry told me about those recs. It doesn't satisfy me, but at least he made the effort to explain it."

Klemm is doing his best to focus on the acceptable elements in both sides of the political dispute and to convince the leaders of each faction that, while he is not an all-out supporter, he is by no means an adversary, either. And, while Klemm is careful about what he says, he does not attempt to bestow a snow job on either of the contenders. He shows enough understanding of both positions to convey to the others that he is reasonable, open-minded, and could still be convinced.

In remaining neutral between the extremes of political contention:

> Understand both positions;
> Listen carefully to learn what people are saying;
> Look for the points in each case with which you can agree;
> Be candid in saying where you have reservations, but emphasize your points of agreement;
> Continually indicate your receptiveness to more argument.

Note one thing. At no point does Walter Klemm say anything like, "I'm not interested. Who needs company politics? I just want to do my job and stay out of it." This attitude, if expressed, does not win allies. It implies a kind of contempt for those who *do* play politics—and since they are likely to be influential parties in the work group, they will not respond kindly to a holier-than-thou position. We hear people repeat the quotation, "A plague on both your houses"; but bear in mind that the fellow who said that was

Mercutio in *Romeo and Juliet*—and within a couple of minutes he was dead.

You may be well advised to pursue an active and flexible middle-of-the-road position, if you are sure that you are not identified with a particular group.

But what if, even without wishing it or doing much to make it happen, you *are* on a particular side?

First of all be objective in sizing up your side's chances if it comes to a showdown. Don't let what you feel or what you want cloud the coolness of your evaluation. If you decide that the side you're on looks like a winner, fine. Stick with it. You don't have to go all out in waving the flag; people who are excessively zealous ultimately make even their closest friends a little uneasy. Just stay firm in the ranks.

Getting Off a Losing Side

But what if you are identified with the faction that looks like a sure loser? Well, it is not our purpose to suggest that anybody turn his back on his most cherished friends or his most deeply held convictions. However, let us say that you are not that active a political partisan; you just happen to be in the wrong clique. If that's the case, then you may want to find a way to get out of that position.

Nancy Karpov had never thought much about the political aspects of her relationships within the department. She just naturally drifted toward a certain group, perhaps because they were more actively looking for supporters. This group, while congenial, spends a lot of time knocking the company and the boss. Nancy has done her share, more to show that she is "with it" than out of deep conviction.

But now Karpov is a little more mature. She's seeing things in a different light. And one of the things she is seeing is the equation between her prospects for keeping her job during a period when the company is cutting back, and the potential danger that her membership in the "anti-company" clique poses for those prospects.

Here's what Nancy Karpov does. She begins to take issue with her acquaintances; not too vehemently, but definitely. She says "It seems to me that we spend a lot of time knocking Mrs. Boomer and the way she runs the place, but we don't come up with too many positive suggestions. Is that really the way to go?"

Karpov continues to take this position, and her friends at first tolerate her, then argue with her, and finally begin to draw away from her. Some of them expect that Nancy will go running to the other gang; but Nancy does no such thing. She bears her solitude in silence, and waits.

One day Del French, one of the more influential members of the "in" crowd, approaches Karpov and suggests a cup of coffee. They get into a discussion of the way things are done in the department. Nancy Karpov by no means agrees with everything that Del French says. In fact she disagrees on a number of points: "No, I can't see that. I think it would be a lot fairer—and more efficient, too—to give everybody a chance to improve their skills on all jobs." And so on.

The conversations continue with French and other members of the potentially stronger faction. And gradually Nancy permits herself to be won over on most points —although not on all. Finally she has gravitated to the group that has the better chance of survival.

Is this betrayal? No. Nancy Karpov betrayed neither individuals nor ideals. If we were to be branded as traitors every time we reached a new stage of our lives and changed our minds about something, all of us would carry that stigma. When we reach a new view of work, life, and our relationships with them, we are entitled to change.

But it has to be done with some finesse. Nancy Karpov began to say things that eventually caused her original group to draw away from her. But she did not actively pursue acceptance into the other group. She waited until she was approached—and then she was no immediate pushover in buying all their ideas.

The essence of the method is not to be too anxious. Psychologists have determined that we place more value on the friendship and the opinions of those whom we have to cultivate, than we do on those who agree with us right away. In making your move from one political faction to another, here's a possible plan to follow:

> Express disagreement with the generally held opinions of the group;
> Continue to disagree, gently, but without making any effort to hide it.
> When the first faction pulls away, don't rush to join the other side.
> When they approach you, be receptive but not eager.
> Permit yourself to be gradually won over.

Shifting sides in a political dispute can be a delicate operation, but it may become a necessary one. With patience and planning, it can be done successfully.

Don't Ostrich It

We have talked about the necessity of becoming attuned to the political forces in your company and your work group. We have made some observations on the strategy of staying between groups, and of changing sides when it becomes obligatory. None of the recommendations here involve either all-out currying of favor or knifing a rival in the back. These are more extreme measures not to be ignored, but which will be discussed in another chapter.

In most organizations there is a political situation. To try to ignore it would be like a fish trying to ignore water. But with thought and skill, you can handle political problems that bear upon your tenure and use them to fortify your grip on your job.

8

Using Colleagues and Subordinates to Strengthen Your Position

You can fortify your hold on your job by mounting your own public relations campaign, or, as the vernacular has it, blowing your own horn—but sweetly. In this sense *public relations* does not mean turning out press releases or holding news conferences or hiring some hotshot writer to compose speeches for you. It means projecting an image of yourself as being valuable to the company in ways that go beyond the job you do. The primary target for your campaign is the boss or bosses who decide on who stays or who goes. But—as is frequently the case in PR—the project works indirectly. You project the right image to the brass hats by influencing the attitudes of your colleagues and/or subordinates.

There are a couple of cornerstones on which the campaign must rest. One is the assumption that you do your job as best you can. Another is that you do not go out of your way to make enemies. Given these basics there are a number of areas into which you can move in projecting the *image of multiplied value,* which can make the difference between staying and going when things get tough.

Become a Resource

Consolidated Cobalt, like many organizations, carries on what they call an "executive training program." The essence of this effort is that supposedly promising young men and women are given some sketchy orientation and then assigned in rotation to the various divisions of the firm.

To most department managers, and to their subordinates, the training program is a pain in the neck, if not elsewhere. Two or three trainees descend upon the operation, almost invariably without any briefing in what is going on. The department head is usually too busy to spend much time with them; so he fobs off the assignment on somebody else. This involuntary trainer does not get time off from his regular work, nor does he get paid more. So he greets the trainees with surly resentment and—as soon as he can—sticks them off in a corner someplace to read a lot of incomprehensible documents.

That's the way it happens most of the time at ConCob. But not in the traffic department. The department manager, Manny Weiss, is just as busy and just as grudging about baby-sitting with trainees as his counterparts. But Weiss is lucky. He has a subordinate, Reg Denker, who seems to like doing this sort of thing.

So Reg Denker always gets the chore of taking care of the trainees. Furthermore Denker—with Weiss's approval —manages to spend some time talking to the people in personnel and training about the best ways to handle these recruits. Personnel has come to think of Reg Denker as practically an unofficial member of the training staff. Weiss doesn't care as long as Denker gets his work done, and this seems to happen. Reg is no ball of fire; he is about average. But he gets by, and still manages to pursue his specialty of working ex officio with the training manager. Consequently he is known in that staff department, and his name is often mentioned.

Reg Denker has made himself a resource to another department of the company. If there is a purge, this does not give him any guarantee of keeping his job while others are fired. But it significantly increases his chances. Denker has seen to it that tributes to his training activities have crept into his file. Furthermore he has established excellent relationships with a growing number of the young managers in the firm. Reg is not necessarily a genius as a trainer, but the people who are compelled to go through this dreary experience are so grateful for a little attention or even a kind word, that they magnify these niceties into superguidance and career assistance. Reg has successfully accomplished the public relations man's dream; he has built himself a favorable image.

Look around for an area in which you can become a resource to others in the company. You don't have to be an expert. The more neglected the service, the greater will be the kudos conferred on you for any assistance at all. Carry on your program as a resource without trying to get it added to your job description or getting a raise on the basis of it. What you are doing will be considered an extra, a bonus. When others feel that they are getting something of value from you without having to pay you for it, they will tend to exert influence to keep you around.

Resolve Conflicts

Sometimes people who work with each other dislike each other. This obvious fact is often overlooked as an opportunity to strengthen job-keeping capability.

Rose Henkel and Doris Schechter are enemies. Every once in a while their enmity breaks out into an open skirmish. A lot of their co-workers welcome these uproars as a diverting interruption in routine. But the boss of the operation, Keith Dowell, does not see it that way. Fights between Rose and Doris cut down on production, and sometimes the fallout can last for as long as a week before the two are making at least a pretense of cooperation. Furthermore neither Rose nor Doris likes to be in a state of active warfare, but neither one is willing to back down.

Here is where Sandra Balkan comes in. Two months ago a squabble erupted between Henkel and Schechter. Instead of watching with amusement the antics of the battlers and the ineffectual efforts of the boss to resolve them, Sandra got into the act. She went over to Rose and said, "Come here, honey. I want to talk to you." Sandra did not do much talking. She listened while Rose got her latest grievance off her chest. Then Sandra went through the same routine with Doris. In far less time than it had previously taken, the two were—while not back on speaking terms—at least working with each other, as a result of Sandra's peacemaking.

Since then Sandra has become an unofficial conflict resolver. She is not a referee; she does not make decisions. But somehow she is able to soothe ruffled feathers and get things back on track.

You can develop facility as a conflict resolver. You are unlikely to run out of raw material; few organizations run entirely free of interpersonal disputes. And it takes no special talent. You don't have to be a Sigmund Freud or a Henry Kissinger—although, like Freud, you have to listen to some wild stuff, and, like Kissinger, you have to keep the parties separate and move from one to the other.

Mostly what it takes is a calm, understanding attitude. Separate the combatants. Listen to one adversary, nod your head, and murmur some soothing things. Then go through the same thing with the other individual. Many people who get into a fight want to blow off steam and then forget about it. This is something that you may be able to do better than the boss; his position makes it more difficult.

Never take sides. And be careful not to go beyond your role as a sympathetic listener unless you are pretty sure that you can accomplish something as a mediator. Mediation, as opposed to just calming the parties down, takes time, experience, and skill—and it's apt to get you more involved than you want to be.

But if you are able to help out your colleagues by doing something to take the steam out of disputes, you will have added a dimension to your image that provides the little "something extra," which may be all it takes to save your job.

Involve Yourself in Long-Term Commitments

The bosses are considering the necessity of firing one of two men. The two—John Zale and George Farmer—have been around about the same length of time. There seems to be little difference in ability. They earn about the same amount of money. They are, of course, different individuals, but neither appears to be any better liked than the other. The bosses are looking for some basis on which to make the unpleasant but necessary decision.

"There's one thing," says the assistant boss. "Zale is involved in something, although I don't know if anything will come of it. You know that for years we have been running into this business of lack of coordination with the gang on the thirteenth floor. Well, Zale got together with a few of the boys down there and has been meeting informally with them, I understand. They expected to have something that might be helpful in about a month."

The big boss asks, "Do you think they'll come up with

anything?" The assistant boss shrugs, "Perhaps not. But, on the other hand, you never know."

The big boss thinks this over. He asks a few more questions. Then: "Well, it strikes me that even if they don't come up with anything useful—and I doubt that they will—this kind of thing ought to be encouraged. We don't have enough interface between departments. It might shake up the thirteenth floor people if John is let go now. Shoot down all the effort that's gone into that project so far. How about George Farmer—is he part of this, too?"

The assistant boss shakes his head no. And although there is still more deliberating to be done, at that moment the die is cast. Poor George Farmer will be the unfortunate who draws the black spot. John Zale has managed to give himself a slight edge that turns out to be decisive.

Like the other approaches suggested in this chapter, this technique is not presented as a block-busting panacea to job-keeping problems. It is, rather, another thing you can do to give yourself a small but potentially important advantage, when and if decisions have to be made about who stays and who goes. The guts of this technique is involvement in a commitment that will stretch beyond the potential firing point.

Such a commitment is most solid when you make it with your boss. For example, by taking on a project in which he is interested and for the completion of which he would be inclined to keep you on the job. But you can't always do that. However, there are ways that you can, on your own, start projects in motion with your colleagues—or subordinates, if you have any—that will serve as an anchor to windward. The project should be something of potential benefit to the organization. It should involve others. The attitude you want to instill in the boss's mind can be expressed in this way: "If I fire him now, it will not only waste the time and effort that he has put into this thing so far, but it will waste the time and effort of the others as well." And so, given that little extra reason for not firing you, he decides that you should stay onboard.

Be a Social Catalyst

Janice Smith says, "I don't know if you've all got the word, but Portia will be retiring at the end of the month. Of course there will be the regular company party for her, with the gift and the whole bit, but it would be nice if we could do something for her ourselves. After all, we've worked with her for a long time, and we all know her, and, well, I think it would be great if we could do something. The trouble is, I'm awfully busy right now, and I just haven't got the time to put it together. Somebody would have to take on the responsibility of raising the money, reserving a place, and seeing that we have a suitable gift and all the rest of it. Naturally it's not part of the job, but I was wondering, would anybody like to do it?"

There is a heavy silence—not unexpected. Then somebody speaks up. "I'll do it," says Mary Burke.

Mary's friends look at her in surprise. Then they look at each other. Has Mary taken leave of her senses? After all it isn't as if Portia were dear to everyone's heart. She's been a good worker, no doubt, but the fact is that very few will miss her. So why has Mary let herself in for the thankless task of organizing the proceedings? It's a lot of extra work, and who needs it?

Mary Burke has volunteered for a variety of reasons, some of which she has not fully thought out. She is no great fan of Portia's, either, but she is embarrassed at the thought that nobody is willing to do anything for a colleague of such longstanding. Along with that Mary feels a little bit guilty; maybe it wasn't altogether Portia's fault that she wasn't popular. Maybe she had troubles they didn't know about, and perhaps if more effort had been made to get to know her, and so on. But along with this—let's face it—Mary has a feeling that volunteering for some extracurricular activity might not hurt her. She reads the papers, she knows about the economic situation, and—while the managers all say there's nothing to worry about—she *is* a little worried about her job. Mary Burke doesn't know whether or not this can help, but it certainly can't hurt.

Burke is right. It can't hurt, and it may very well help.

Business firms are also social institutions. People of varying personalities, backgrounds, needs, and problems spend a considerable amount of time with each other, joined in a mutual enterprise. Since human beings are social animals, there must be a certain amount of give-and-take involving interpersonal amenities having nothing to do—officially, at least—with the work.

And people want to work in harmony. They like to have fun at work. They enjoy being nice to others and to just socialize with their colleagues. Bosses like to see this happen, when it doesn't get in the way of the job.

But organized social amenity requires effort. It takes somebody to act as catalyst and to put it together. And most of us have developed a healthy aversion to volunteering for that kind of assignment. Many of us think of it as a thankless job.

It is not thankless. Colleagues are grateful to the person who is willing to do it. Sometimes that gratefulness may be expressed in a kidding way—"Do you mean to tell me you're going to hang around here and do all that extra work on the picnic? You need your head examined!"—but the gratitude is there nevertheless. People sense that *someone* has to do it; the workplace would be dull indeed without social give-and-take. So they welcome the willingness of the individual who will do it.

Being the social catalyst for your work group does not always mean taking up collections or organizing lunches or bowling parties or picnics. A lot of the most enjoyable work-connected socializing is spontaneous. But it takes somebody to look around, smile, and say, "Who wants to take a trip over to the zoo at lunchtime?" Not everyone is in the mood for spur-of-the-moment fun. That's fine; it is not compulsory to participate. But everyone will like the idea that there is someone who can usually be counted on to get something going.

All it takes to become the social catalyst is willingness, good humor, and a capacity to enjoy life. You get to know people better and have more fun around the job. But even more important, you may be assuring yourself of continuing employment. Companies and work groups want to keep people who make things pleasant. A lot of real-life counterparts to Mary Burke are still working today because of this fact.

Provide a Reservoir of Information

Every organization has a history. Embedded in that history are decisions and customs that are remnants of the past. Newer additions to the staff are only vaguely aware of them and don't know what they mean.

But sometimes people want to know. A supervisor, Andy Kiner, is examining a chart. He points to a section of it and asks "See this cutout here? I never noticed it before this morning, but, sure enough, it's there in the wall, just covered up, that's all. Anybody know what it's for?"

Nobody knows. Kiner says, "The reason I'm wondering is that maybe we could use it to run some leads through there for those big pumps. Things would be a hell of a lot easier if we could. But I hate to go in there not knowing what the cutout is for. I could go to engineering, but you know how that is. Take them three days to dig out all the prints. If we only knew what the damn thing is doing there we could be surer of what we're doing."

Somebody has an idea: "Let's ask Joe Chaikin." Kiner immediately agrees.

Who is Joe Chaikin? Well, he's just a guy; he doesn't even work in the department. But Joe Chaikin has built up a reputation as knowing a great many odd facts about the company, the people who have worked there, and the buildings in which they worked.

It's not that Chaikin is a real old-timer. He's been around for six years or so, that's all. But he seems to have a knack for storing information, and so he's the man they ask when there's a question nobody else can answer. And, sure enough, Joe Chaikin is able to help. "The way I understand it—and this was long ago, before my time—they were going to put a plating machine in here. They got the plant all ready, but then the contract didn't come through. It was a government contract, I think. . . ." Andy Kiner hears enough to form a more definite idea about whether or not he can make use of his discovery.

It's interesting to find out all you can about the place you work. And it makes you a more interesting and useful colleague, even for people who don't work directly with you. Your reputation as a fount of information will spread. You will acquire an image as somebody who is willing and able to come up with answers that nobody else has got. Along with that, you will be seen as somebody who is so thoroughly identified with the company as to have become part of its continuing growth and development.

It's tough to fire someone who has become part of the company tradition.

Using Your Enemies
The strategies outlined above all involve a certain amount

of harmony and cooperation with colleagues and subordinates. The assumption is that you like to get along with people and that you are able to keep your accumulation of enemies to a minimum.

But let's say there are a number of people who hate you. We won't go into the reasons why this might happen. At first glance such a situation is by no means an auspicious one for job retention—but there may be ways you can turn it to your advantage.

Bill Mallow had a run-in with the guys in quality control about six months ago. The friction has continued. There are people in the other division who constantly say unpleasant things about Bill's personality, probity, antecedents, and eating habits. The animosity just seems to go on and on.

Bill Mallow goes to his boss. "Steve," he says, "I can fight my own battles and I don't want to get you involved in this. You've got enough to worry about. All I want to ask is, do you think I'm wrong?"

The boss assures Mallow that, as far as he can see, Mallow is in the right. Mallow says, "That's all I wanted to hear. You can be sure that, if this thing goes on, it won't be because I keep it going. I'm just interested in doing the best job I can. In fact I'm motivated to do a better job than I ever did before. I'll be damned if I will be responsible for giving those guys a legitimate chance to take potshots at us."

Mallow keeps the boss out of the battle. But he does keep the boss informed: "They'd sure like to nail us. But this department is turning out such good runs that they can't find an opening. We're making them look like monkeys."

Bill Mallow is using his enemies to help solidify his hold on his job. While the boss has not been drawn into the dispute, he is aware of it. Not unnaturally, he would not want to do anything that would seem to be knuckling under to critics. So even if he is under pressure to lay off Mallow, he will be reluctant to do so, because Bill Mallow has become a symbol of resistance to unfair sniping.

It's better not to make enemies. But if you do, you may want to think about the possibility of making them work for you. If you can convince your boss that their antagonism toward you is really antagonism toward the operation—including him—you may be able to at least neutralize the disadvantage of your unpopularity and even turn it to your advantage.

Your image as it is seen by other people may not exactly correspond to the way you really are. Most people's images become somewhat distorted as they are projected to a larger audience, like your colleagues and subordinates. Nevertheless that image may be influential in helping to determine how well you're able to hang on to your job. So the idea is not to just trust to luck, but to do something about shaping the image in a way that reflects you favorably. That's what PR is all about.

We have reviewed a number of image-projecting techniques. We have talked of them, on the whole, as ways in which you can use your colleagues in the company to strengthen your job grip. With modifications most of these approaches can be applied to your subordinates, if you happen to boss others.

With the exception of the last plan—making use of your enemies—the suggestions are keyed to helpfulness. When you make yourself helpful to others in a number of small ways, and you work this way with enough people, you begin to build up a balance on your side. If the unhappy moment comes when you are considered as a candidate for termination, all of these little things, added together, can add weight to the half of the balance that comes down in favor of you.

There are always opportunities to make yourself pleasant and helpful to other people. We have offered a few. As you examine the scene, you will spot many more. It takes some effort, usually, but the payoff in increased security can make it more than worthwhile.

9

Outside Strings You Can Pull

I was up in Westport visiting my cousin," Larry Prentice tells his boss. "He said he expected to be placing a large order for our new food blender next week."

The sentence seems casual enough, even offhand. But it carries an implicit message to Larry's boss: "Just remember that I'm related to and on good terms with one of our best customers." It's a bit of information that will obviously be a strong factor for Larry Prentice's continued employment, no matter *how tough* the going may become for his firm.

Remember the advertising campaign used by an airline a few years ago: "If you have it, flaunt it!"? The same idea that attracted passengers to that airline can serve notice on an employer that an employee has outside connections that can be used both in the company's favor or against it.

Having an "in" with your employer's customers is always a reinforcing factor. And, of course, you don't have to be a relative. Employees have gotten the same kind of mileage from being friends, neighbors, or even college pals of customers, key suppliers, and so on.

Making the Connection

If you don't already have a helpful contact with people on the outside with whom it's important for your employer to have good relations, you can set about developing them. And, of course, your targets are not confined to any one group. There are other connections you can have that may work strongly in your favor:

Customers. They are always a particularly strong help.

Suppliers. Sometimes firms that sell goods or services to your employer can be a good source. These contacts can be especially helpful when the materials or services they provide are in short supply.

Mutual friends. In some cases your boss or someone higher up in the organization may have a friend who is also yours. Tactful development of this situation can be a leverage point for you.

The boss's family. You don't have to marry the boss's daughter to gain special status. Being a friend in good standing with the boss's immediate family or relatives can obviously yield desirable benefits.

Experts in the field. In some cases employers are in a technical field in which there are individuals whose expertness is generally acknowledged. Your friendliness or even contacts with people of this kind can be helpful to you. A typical method for developing such contacts: attendance at trade conventions, industry exhibitions, membership in professional groups, and so on.

Your own participation in "trade" activities. One young engineer was able to improve his situation considerably by doing a series of articles that were published in one of the better-known trade journals in his field. Another employee with a gift for public speaking was able to develop two or three interesting talks involving areas of interest in his industry, which got him included in panel discussions and as a guest speaker in industry and professional meetings.

How It Works

Having or developing these outside contacts can do several things for you, if—and only if—they are *properly used.*

In one case, as in the anecdote that started this chapter, it's clear that an employee whose goodwill can favorably influence sales or make any other improvement in company operations, packs real clout. However, in other cases you may not be able to bring pressure that's as strong or obvious in your favor. But what can and does happen is that the kind of contacts we've been talking about on the outside gives you high visibility. It makes you a standout among your colleagues. And this in turn gets you special and favorable attention when people are being evaluated for any reason.

How well you do as a result of having outside contacts depends in part on how skillfully you use them. For example, it's possible to play a hand badly: Steve Kyle was a golf-playing buddy of one of his firm's better customers. This was a fact that he crammed down his boss's throat at every opportunity. His boss managed to hold on to his resentment for some time, but one day, finally annoyed and fed up, he blew up when Kyle overplayed his hand: "Steve, I don't care if your golf buddy is head of General Motors or even if he's our best customer—which he isn't. But I can tell you this: If our good relations with him depend on you, I'd rather lose him as a customer than continue to put up with this line you've been dishing out."

The boss was taking a gamble, but probably one he could win. When the chips were down, the customer was unlikely to stop buying on the say-so of a not-too-bright Steve Kyle.

The effectiveness of outside contacts really lies in their

implicit value. Mentioned tactfully, used gracefully—and as often as possible to help the company—they can be a very strong and favorable factor in one's company career.

It's only when *too much* weight is attributed to them that the bubble may burst. Perhaps the best way to use contacts of this kind is just to take the steps necessary to let them be known in your company, especially with your boss. But then let matters rest right there.

As we mentioned earlier, if you can use these contacts in a positive way to help your company, you're strengthening their value. But if these contacts are not easily converted into obvious company benefits, you have to let them tell their own story for whatever it's worth. And, as we've been pointing out, that can be a great deal.

The "Inside" Outsider—the Consultant

The consultant is a familiar figure on the business scene. There are all kinds of consultants, and companies call on them for all sorts of things. Sometimes they ask a consultant who should be fired.

So it's a good idea to *be kind to the consultant.* This obviously applies in the case of the expert who is advising the boss on how to reorganize the operation, or on matters of personnel. This breed of consultant may not be too accessible to you; you may not even know he's there. He certainly does not wear a sign reading "I can recommend that you be fired." If he visits the workplace he may be introduced in general terms as somebody who is working on some vague project, or he may be given a cover story. The outsider who comes around to "study methods of eliminating paperwork" may really be preparing a report that will lead to changes in the staff. You can't tell; so it's best to assume that any outside expert may have some influence on your job tenure.

Consultants need information. They have to talk to the

people who do the work. A lot of people clam up when the consultant arrives. They seem to go on the assumption that "the less he knows about me, the less he can use against me." Wrong. You are much better off if you talk freely to the consultant, tell him what he wants to know, and explain what you do in your job with a show of expertise and enthusiasm.

This kindness to the consultant can help you in a number of ways. For one thing he will be grateful to the person who treats him like a human being and helps him do his job. Then, while he may be evaluating you, he is certainly likely to be somewhat impressed if you seem to know what you are talking about and if you act enthusiastically about the company and the job. When he does not know anything about a worker, he may be more likely to conclude that that worker is expendable—particularly if the project calls for him to recommend that some people be cut.

There's one more point. If you are a useful source of information to the expert, he may tend to feel that you will be a good person to have around, if and when he comes in to do further consulting work in the company (and all consultants hope to be asked back).

Even if the consultant is not making recommendations on personnel policy, his good opinion can be useful. If an expert who is studying, say, materials-handling techniques happens to mention in his report that he received good cooperation from you, you have chalked up a plus with management. In fact, after you've been helpful to a consultant, you might well ask him to put in a good word for you. Why not?

A boost from a consultant usually carries weight with the bosses, since consultants are considered to be people who see vast numbers of organizations and develop a keen eye for talent. So when the expert looms upon the scene, look upon him as an opportunity, not as a threat.

10

The Law: It May
Protect Your Job

THE unquestioned right of the boss to fire a worker—once
a universal staple of the system—has been reduced
significantly over the past fifty years. That "right" continues to erode. As it stands now, the majority of workers
have some legal protection—at least on paper—against
being fired unfairly or maliciously. This development grows
out of the spread of unionism, a couple of landmark pieces
of federal legislation, and, more recently, some interesting
court decisions.

We're not suggesting that the average employee who
faces imminent termination can hold on to his job through
legal action. However, as we will see, sometimes it can be
helpful just to let the boss know that you are aware of the
possibility of legal action.

The Federal Laws
You can't be fired because you are of a particular race or

religion, because you're a woman, or because you're over forty. It's the law.

There are two legislative cornerstones to this proposition:

Title VII of the Civil Rights Act of 1964 prohibits job discrimination based on race, color, religion, sex, or national origin. It applies to employers engaged in an industry affecting commerce who have at least twenty-five employees on each working day in twenty or more weeks of the year. It applies also to labor unions. It does not include specified government agencies, U. S.-Government-owned corporations, religious and educational institutions, private membership clubs other than labor unions, or Indian tribes.

The Age Discrimination in Employment Act of 1967 prohibits job discrimination based on age. It protects people who are at least forty but under sixty-five, working in companies similar to those specified in the Civil Rights Act of 1964.

Both of these acts cover firing as a possible discriminatory act. There is one other piece of legislation that is worth mentioning: the Equal Pay Act. This law covers wages; it may be applicable in cases where a company tries to force resignation by reducing pay.

The Age Discrimination Act is enforced by the Wage and Hour Division of the U. S. Labor Department, as is the Equal Pay Act. Title VII of the 1964 Civil Rights Act is enforced by the Equal Employment Opportunity Commission (EEOC).

There are teeth in these laws. Businessmen are still in the process of learning just how sharp these teeth may be, and where they are likely to bite.

Here, in brief, are a couple of examples of how the Age Discrimination Act works. The Hickok Manufacturing Company fired fifty-six-year-old Charles Schulz, a district sales manager. They said that Schulz was not doing his job satisfactorily.

Schulz brought action under the age-discrimination law. The company was unable to produce sufficient evidence of Schulz's lack of competence. The Federal District Court ruled in favor of Schulz, ordering the company to reinstate him in his former position or a comparable one and pay him two and one-half years back pay.

Standard Oil of California fired 160 employees, ranging from managers and engineers to gas station attendants. They were all between forty and sixty-five. The company said the reason was "declining manpower requirements." However, a case was brought and the government claimed it saw a pattern of discrimination against older employees. Standard Oil of California did not admit to having broken the law, but they agreed to a settlement involving $2 million in back wages and to the rehiring of three-quarters of the fired employees.

There is a sizable government apparatus to process complaints under the job discrimination laws. In recent years, while other federal departments have been cut back, the EEOC has received larger appropriations. In 1974 there were more than 900 compliance officers in ten regions around the country to investigate charges, and they have a full workload. By mid-1974, for example, more than 14,000 complaints of age discrimination had been filed with the Labor Department.

Is the Employer Safe in Laying Off According to Seniority?

Companies are finding that, "I did it according to seniority," is not an infallible defense against charges of discrimination in firing. The courts disagree. The confusion extends to workers covered by union contracts as well as to those who are not.

For example, take the case of *Jersey Central Power & Light Co.* v. *Local 327, International Brotherhood of Electrical Workers, CCA-3, 1/30/75.* The company was laying off workers according to seniority. When a suit was brought, a federal district court ruled that the union contract's seniority provisions could not be allowed to frustrate the goals of an EEOC agreement setting certain minority and female ratios in the company's ranks. But the U. S. Third Circuit Court of Appeals overturned the lower court ruling, holding that to ignore seniority provisions simply to ease the impact of layoffs on minorities would be "reverse discrimination."

There are other rulings that support those of the circuit court. However, the question is apt to remain cloudy for some time. Two things, though, become clear. The courts are "invading" to a greater and greater extent the "traditional prerogative" of the employer in deciding who stays and who goes. Furthermore the courts are tending to look at the whole picture. If there is a past pattern of discrimination, seniority may not be acceptable as the cardinal rule governing layoffs.

The employer can always cite "business necessity" as a reason for making firing decisions. But the employer may have to prove business necessity. And even if he can show that bona fide business considerations were an important factor in a termination, he still may not win the case.

For example, in *Laugeson* v. *The Anaconda Co.*, *CA-6, #73-2205, 1/10/75,* a Circuit Court of Appeals ruled that business considerations were not decisive because age was *at least one factor*—although a secondary one—in the decision to fire. The company had provided ample evidence that economic difficulties had compelled it to cut back. The lower-court judge instructed the jury that they should uphold the charge of discrimination only if they found that age was the *sole* reason for firing.

But the higher court said that this was too strict a definition of the law: "Even though the need to reduce the employee force generally was also a strong, and perhaps even more compelling, reason, the employee is nevertheless entitled to recover damages if one such factor was his age. . . ."

If a discharged worker falls into one (or more) of the categories designated in the laws, he may have grounds for a complaint. And the employer cannot be sure that reasons of seniority or business necessity will always prevail.

Can They Force You to Retire Early?

Early retirement can be a reasonably attractive recourse for employers who have to cut down the payroll. A good many employees welcome this resolution of the problem.

But they can't force you into early retirement if you are not enrolled in a bona fide employment benefit that mandates early retirement. The plan has to be in existence, the employee must be aware of it and be a participant in it, and he should receive benefits from it. Such plans cannot be erected as devices to get around the Age Discrimination in Employment Act. And they should not be discriminatory. Some plans may involve different benefits, requirements, and treatment for women as against men. This is a violation of the Civil Rights Act of 1964.

An employer cannot force a worker into early retirement—even if he has a bona fide plan—if that worker does not participate in the plan. American Hardware Mutual Insurance Co. had a plan mandating retirement for women at sixty-two and men at sixty-five. Although participation was optional, the company had long followed the practice of retiring all female employees at sixty-two, whether they were enrolled in the plan or not. One non-participating woman challenged the rule and won her case.

The Contract You Didn't Know You Had

Few of us sign contracts in taking jobs. But a contract does not have to be in writing to be binding. Courts are beginning to remind employers and employees of this fact in some dramatic ways.

The traditional way of looking at it has been that, if there is nothing in writing, there is no obligation. Many bosses assume this to be the case, and most employees go on that assumption as well.

But let's take a look at *Lucas* v. *Whittaker Corp.*, 335 F. *Supp. 889*. The employee had been with his previous firm for nine years. He moved his family from Missouri to Colorado to take a new job after an oral offer of employment for two years. He was fired after thirteen months. He sued and won the remaining eleven months' pay. The court ruled that the oral promise had caused the employee to make serious changes in his life, and that the company had to deliver on the promise.

Another employee (*Doody* v. *John Sexton & Co., 411 F 2d 1119*) moved his family across the country in response to the employer's promise of "lifetime employment." He was fired. He sued for out-of-pocket expenses of $15,000 and won. The employer pleaded that he was "just kidding" about a lifetime job, but the court held that this was fraudulent misrepresentation, and that the employee was reasonable in assuming that the boss was serious.

In judging the validity of oral promises, courts are taking into account the trouble to which the employee goes to take the new job. It isn't necessary for the employee to have moved a great distance. If he has given up a good job to take the new one, he may have a basis for successful action.

It has been traditional to regard employment that does not involve a written contract as being "at will"; either party can terminate the relationship when he wishes. However, a case in New Hampshire has given a startling jolt to that assumption.

Olga Monge worked for the Beebe Rubber Company.

After three months she applied for a higher-paying job. The foreman indicated she could have the job if she were "nice." Soon after she got the better job, the foreman asked her for a date. Ms. Monge—married with three children—refused.

Not long after this she was put on another machine at a much lower rate of pay. Her overtime was cut off. Then the foreman consented to reinstate her overtime if she would sweep floors and clean out rest rooms. (It might be pointed out that Ms. Monge, formerly a schoolteacher in Costa Rica, was attending college five nights a week in pursuit of a teaching degree and working night shift at the rubber company.)

Olga Monge was fired. She sued for breach of contract. The jury awarded her damages and the New Hampshire Supreme Court upheld the decision, saying that evolving legal, economic, and social conditions warranted the switch from "settled law." The decision stated that it is in the public interest to strike a balance between the employer's business interest and the employee's job security. Henceforth, even without a contract, the employer would be liable for breach of contract if he fired an employee out of bad faith, malice, or retaliation.

In a similar ruling the Indiana Supreme Court held against an employer who fired an employee because she filed a workmen's compensation claim, declaring that the relationship was like that of landlord and tenant.

The potential implications of these rulings are heavy, particularly if they set a trend. In general it would seem that we are coming to a legal situation in which the "at-will" privilege of the employer to fire is of dubious validity, if it is exercised captiously or maliciously. Employers have obligations to workers, even in the *absence* of a written contract.

And the boss cannot smooth his path by alleging

misconduct on the part of the fired worker. If he does, he leaves himself open for a defamation suit.

Knowing the Law Can Help You Keep Your Job

None of this is meant to imply that anybody has a legal right to hold on to his job. However, the trends that militate against the employer's right to fire "at will" in any or all situations can be used as part of your job-keeping strategy.

This book is about how to keep a job, not what to do after you have lost it. Obviously we are not suggesting that every worker in danger of getting fired arm himself with legal counsel. For one thing, no action can be brought until after the firing has taken place. Furthermore the bringing of such an action can be a long, frustrating, expensive, and painful procedure. An older executive who was fired told us: "I have been attempting to invoke the law on Age Discrimination since it was the basis of my firing last year. I am currently wending my way through the corridors of the U. S. Department of Labor, Wage & Hour Division, also trying to untangle the red tape at the (state) Division of Civil Rights. It's, of course, a long, slow process. . . . The paperwork mounts steadily." The experience is typical, costly, and frustrating.

But bear in mind that the process is tortuous and laborious for the employer as well. The larger firm, with lawyers on the payroll or on retainer, is better able to handle it. But no employer welcomes a job-discrimination suit, even when he is sure that the suit has no basis in fact. The paperwork mounts up for managers who must document the company's case. There are reams of questionnaires to fill out. Government enforcement people nose into the nooks and crannies of the organization. And there is the concurrent problem that, in hard times, courts are apt to bend over backward to protect the employee's right to earn a living.

So the employer has every reason to shudder at the mere suggestion of a job-discrimination action in court. And this can work to your advantage.

There are two basic steps you can take. First, begin to prepare your documentation. Assume that, if you are fired, the company will give a reason that will fall into one of two categories, or will straddle both. One reason is economic conditions; they can't afford to keep you on the payroll. The other possible reason is less-than-complete delivery on job requirements.

Become familiar with how the company is actually making out—as against what management might be saying. Is the industry really suffering? What have earnings and profits been like? Are upper-management figures taking cuts or being pruned from the roster? Who has gotten raises recently, and where do they stand in the organization? What steps have been taken to give the company better economic stability? Are they trying to cut costs in other areas?

As to your own performance, measure yourself against others who do similar work. To the extent that what you do is reflected in numbers, compare your output against that of your colleagues. Save any indication of the company's favor (a congratulatory note on a job you did, for example). If possible, try to obtain recognition of any achievements in writing. Meanwhile consider what documentation the company might produce if it were called upon to prove that you were not doing an adequate job. How strong is it? (How strong is the *documentation*, not the objective fact. Maybe you did louse something up, but can they prove it?) Look for the patterns the company follows, not just in firing but in promotion, pay, hiring, etc. Could a pattern be discerned if you were looking for it? Might you fit into the category of one who is being discriminated against in any way? Has an angry boss ever said anything to you or about you that could be interpreted as reflecting bias?

This amassing of documentation would, of course, come into play if you were discharged and decided to bring suit. But it may, under certain circumstances, help to influence the employer in favor of keeping you on the job.

Because the other basic element of your use of the legal position is to let the boss know you are thinking about it. Some bosses tend to assume that employees don't know about these recourses: the federal regulations, the state cases regarding the employment contract, etc. If an employer becomes aware that a particular worker is up-to-date on the possibilities of legal action inherent in the situation, he may be swayed somewhat in a direction away from firing. His unwillingness to risk the costs and time of a lawsuit—let alone the possibility of an unfavorable (to him) decision—might make the difference in impelling him to decide to keep you on the job.

Here's how one employee handled the tactic of letting the boss know she had certain things on her mind. Verna Pilgrim is talking with her department manager, Jo Stewart. Recently a couple of people were fired from another division of the firm. Verna says, "I was sorry to see Louise go."

Stewart allows as how she was sorry, too, but that's the way things happen sometimes. Verna sticks with the topic: "It surprises me that Louise isn't making a federal case out it. Of course, maybe she is and we just don't know about it."

Stewart asks what Verna means. "Well, after all, why was Louise picked out to be fired? As far as I could see her work was just as good as anybody else's over there. And there doesn't seem to be any other big reason. From what I can see, I would think Louise would have a complaint about discrimination, either because of her age or because she's a woman. There are laws that cover these things, and I heard of a case recently where somebody was let go for what seems like more reason than Louise's firing, and she won her case. The company had to take her back and give her back pay and the whole works."

Pilgrim goes on to spell out some of her knowledge of the possible legal situation covering firing. Then she adds, "Naturally I don't know all the circumstances involved in Louise's case. But it seems to me that she might have something going for her there. Maybe she just didn't know about it, in which case the company is lucky. Of course I've always been treated fairly and I don't see any reason why I won't continue to be, but if I had been in Louise's shoes I think I'd have talked to a lawyer, or to the government agency, or somebody."

Verna Pilgrim has gotten her point across. Jo Stewart has been given a little something to think about and to relay up the line. And if it comes to the crunch and the company is considering possibilities for termination, they may feel somewhat apprehensive about taking a chance on letting Verna go.

Keeping a job should not be a function of legal action or the threat of such action, implied or otherwise. And certainly there should be no law that requires an employer to keep on paying an incompetent or a goldbrick. But if an employee is doing his best, and his best has been satisfactory, he would seem to be justified in thinking about angles of leverage that can give him the slight edge needed to retain the job.

If you do get fired, and you think it may be unfair, you

can talk to a lawyer or to the Wage-Hour Division or the Equal Employment Opportunity Commission. The government agencies are in major population centers and are listed in the phone book.

The trick is not to have it come to that. The growing pressure of federal laws and court decisions has placed an additional potential burden on employers to have legitimate reasons for firing people. There is nothing unfair in the requirement that terminations be based on tangible bases. As an outgrowth of this, the possibility of legal action may provide you with one more tactic for self-protection. And this is protection of your right to *do* your job, not your right *not* to do it.

11

Why You Shouldn't Worry about the Other Guy

T HIS is a psychological fact of life that was brought home to the public most clearly during the Vietnam war. Here's a typical case in point: Bert Clarke went through some of the worst days of the Tet offensive. After a while the tides of battle receded and Bert's infantry group—forty men—was resting on the side of a hill. Suddenly a large body of the enemy appeared from the surrounding woods. In the exchange of fire Bert's entire group was almost wiped out. Bert Clarke was one of a handful of survivors. After several weeks in the field hospital, the wound in his arm began to heal, but Bert began suffering from nightmares and anxiety. After several visits to the psychotherapist attached to the medical unit, he knew in general what was wrong: He was suffering a severe sense of guilt. He felt it was unfair that he should have survived when so many of his buddies had died in the battle.

Some people call this the survival syndrome. It occurs

away from the battlefield. People who live through a catastrophe—a boat sinking, an avalanche, an apartment-house fire—that takes many lives but spares theirs, tend to develop deep symptoms of guilt.

The parallel between these instances of survival and people on the work scene who keep their jobs while others—their friends, colleagues—lose theirs, tends to create some kind of destructive feeling. It's the purpose of this chapter to prevent this type of self-accusation, whether conscious or unconscious, to minimize a basic fact that perhaps should give you satisfaction—namely, that you've succeeded in your objective of holding on to your job.

The point is that, unlike a natural disaster or the fortunes of war, there *is* an answer to the *why* that "survivors" ask themselves. And it's the answer to this *why* that can ease your conscience and make you happy to accept your own good fortune:

1. *It's the company's considered choice.* Again, unlike the sequences of events that lead to a natural tragedy, the developments that have led to your surviving a layoff are more or less a rational process. Chances are you've *earned* the right—particularly if you followed the advice in this book—to retain your job. Unlike other considerations that give birth to the survival syndrome, in your case there is a *reason* and probably a good one that explains what's happened. It's the existence of a rational process, the fact that you have won out because someone has thought that you deserved to, that rids the situation of its incomprehensibility. The Viet survivor asks why and there's no answer. The survivor of a roster-cutting operation has done so because his organization decided it was desirable.

2. *Should you have warned the other person?* "I was pretty sure that Henry and Grace were going to get the ax,"

an employee says. "They didn't seem to be aware of what was coming. Should I have warned them?"

The implication here, too, is one of guilt. The feeling might be summed up in the sentence, "I could have warned them, but I didn't."

But the answer here is that it's wise not to pass along a warning for two reasons. First of all, unless you're absolutely sure—and here you would have to be the employee's superior rather than a colleague—you might be making a serious mistake through a misunderstanding. And second, since you could do nothing about it, you might only be precipitating a premature crisis. An employee, warned that he's going to be fired, naturally will rush in to see his boss to find out what's up. It's quite likely that without this unexpected development, the boss could have done a much more tactful and constructive job of letting the employee go than is possible if the interview is approached with anger or misunderstanding by the employee. Here are a couple of thumbnail case histories that show some of the other possible combinations: Manager Ann Farley hears something through her boss's open doorway that leads her to think that a fellow manager, Pearl Bryce, is going to be fired. She calls Pearl at home that night and, with the best of intentions, tells her that she's due to be separated from the company. Pearl Bryce is startled and upset but doesn't say anything. Meanwhile days pass, finally weeks, and nothing happens. Ann Farley finally says, "I'm awfully sorry, Pearl, I guess I misunderstood."

"You sure did," says Pearl Bryce, and that ends their friendship.

Ted Walters knows there's going to be a cut in the staff of advertising copywriters, of which he's a member. Thinking about the situation, he thinks it's pretty clear that Bill

Leeds, newest man in the group, is going to be asked to leave. Feeling friendly toward Bill, Ted tells him, "It isn't final yet, Bill, but it looks bad. If I were you I'd start looking for another job."

Next week, sure enough, two of the staff are let go. But, lo and behold, Bill Leeds isn't one of the two, and Ted Walters is.

Bill Leeds is pretty mad at Ted Walters. He steps into Walters's office, his faced flushed with anger, and says: "It didn't work, did it? You thought you'd panic me into looking for another job. Well, I'm glad you got what was coming to you."

3. *Should you play the Good Samaritan?* There's another way in which people sometimes get into trouble: They learn that someone is going to be fired and then, again possibly with the best of intentions, the thought comes, I'll try to help. I'll put in a good word with the boss.

Again the person with this humane tendency certainly deserves commendation, but consider the possible consequences: Harry Macon learns that two people from the typist pool are going to be let go. The volume of work has fallen off to the point where their services are no longer needed. One of the separated typists is Betty Cole, with whom Harry Macon has become somewhat friendly. He decides to talk to Alice Rice, the head of the typing pool.

Understandably Alice resents the approach. "Listen, Mr. Macon, I want you to understand a couple of things. I don't like to fire anybody. When I finally made my decision, it was after considerable thought, and I'll thank you to mind your own business and let me mind mine. Now will you please leave my office. I have a lot of work to do."

There is only one situation in which this type of interference is justifiable. Putting in a good word for an esteemed colleague isn't it. However, if you have some information not known to the person whose responsibility it was to select the firee, then perhaps you can act. Just make sure that your evidence is both relevant and persuasive. Otherwise you'll find yourself in the same thankless situation as Harry Macon.

4. *Should you pull a Sidney Carton?* As every school-child knows, Sidney Carton was the hero of Dickens's *A Tale of Two Cities,* who sacrifices himself to save the life of the sweetheart of the woman he loved. He substituted himself for Charles Darnay and went serenely off to the guillotine with the satisfaction that he had done a great and good deed.

If you are a bachelor with an independent source of income, or you have the comforting feeling that you'll always make it and your rival has six kids and an ailing wife, and you know one of you has got to go, you may want to help by taking yourself out of the action.

Even if you're not financially independent, you may feel that you need the job so much less than the other fellow that you may want to volunteer to leave, so that he can hold his job. But if this is your inclination, our recommendation is that you don't quit until you get another job first.

Your Own Future

There is another dimension to this proposition of worrying about the other guy. You want to keep your job. You also want to move on to bigger and better things. An attitude of extreme concern for your colleagues may not result in the loss of your job. It may even win you acclaim as a big-hearted person. But it is not likely to enhance your chances for promotion.

Jeff Armbrister became very upset when heads began to roll in his company. He spent time with his boss, not lobbying for himself, but putting in good words for others.

The boss, who respected Jeff's judgment, listened. He was impressed by Jeff's unselfishness and, to some extent, swayed by his arguments.

As it happened a few people were let go. Jeff was not among them. He felt good about having worked to save the jobs of others. But Jeff did not realize the effect that his efforts had had on his own prospects.

A couple of months after the crisis subsided, the company was looking for somebody to promote into a management capacity. Jeff Armbrister appeared on paper to be the leading candidate. He had the brains and the experience.

But Jeff's boss, and his counterparts in top management, were concerned. "Jeff is a nice guy," said one, "and he sure was willing to lay it on the line in support of his friends, and even some guys who were not his friends. But that's what worries me. If we give Jeff this job, can we be sure that he'll have the right management attitude? After all there will be some hard-boiled decisions to make. We can't have a man in that spot who is going to agonize over personnel shifts or over letting people go. Do we want to take that chance?"

The job eventually went to another fellow, one who had battled to keep his own job during the crunch. Jeff never knew why he lost out.

Watch Out for Rumors and Alarms

Any organization that is about to fire some of its employees usually begins to quiver and quake in a nonliteral way. At any rate people begin to feel destructive vibes and look about speculatively for some word on what's up.

Two suggestions can help you weather this type of situation with greater equanimity: Think of yourself. One of the troubles is that a lot of worry is wasted by a lot of people in an unrealistic concern about other people. Sure, it's always bad when people who want to hold on to a job have to leave it. But if you want to be concerned about the world's wars, there are certainly worse situations worthy of your attention: Famine in some parts of the world that's killing innocent people; war that's killing soldier and civilian alike.

It's not illogical for people to be concerned about the unhappy developments in their immediate surroundings. But it's always wrong—that is, in the sense of being unproductive or unhelpful—to try to worry *for* other people. Selfishness may not always be exemplary, but it has a perfectly sound basis in our psychological and biological heritage. Altruism, a regard for the interests of other creatures, exists in nature among many animal species, but the effect of that concern shouldn't magnify the extent of the trouble. After all, for the person who's going to be fired it's no worse a development if he's the only one to be let go or if he's one of several.

In this case of holding on to a job, there's a great deal to be said in favor of *enlightened selfishness*. It keeps things in perspective.

12

Extreme Solutions

WHAT is your job worth? How far are you willing to go to try to keep it?

The job-keeping measures suggested in previous chapters have been more or less work-oriented. They have focused on the ways in which you can make yourself more valuable, give yourself that slight edge that can make all the difference, or build up your image around the work scene as someone who should be retained rather than let go.

Often a campaign that incorporates these elements will work. But sometimes it will not. That is the point at which we may begin to think about more far-out methods, which have less—and sometimes nothing—to do with how we handle ourselves on and around the job.

This book is not a sermon or an exercise in uplift. There are plenty of books that purport to tell you how to cope with life's adversities, including the loss of a job. There are plenty of people who will proclaim that you should not compromise your principles or self-respect by one iota to keep a job ("Nothing is worth that."). In general we agree. But the decision on how far we will go to continue collecting a paycheck is one for each individual to make.

Take the hypothetical case of John Doe, who could save his job by simply apologizing about something to the boss. John Doe, however, insists that he has nothing to apologize for. He was in the right; the boss was in the wrong. So he remains adamant and loses his job.

A lot of people will commend John Doe. "He stuck up for his principles," they will say. But if a collection were taken up to assist this admirable person, a great many people would probably be out to lunch. And, we might ask, what about John Doe's wife, and the eleven-year-old who needs $3,000 worth of dental work, and the needs of the Doe family for at least subsistence-level income? It may well be that the greater courage lies in doing whatever has to be done to try to preserve the job rather than in preserving a self-image.

So here are some comments on a few of the more extreme techniques that can be used when it appears the job is slipping away. You may not want to use any of them; but if they are used, they might as well be used effectively.

Organized Sacrifice

Not long ago New York City faced the necessity of laying off a number of policemen. Those who would feel the ax were the rookies who had just come through the police academy. The Policemen's Benevolent Association came up with an alternate solution. Against some initial opposition, the leadership of the union finally won agreement on a plan by which all cops would sacrifice some paid holiday time to save money, and thus save the jobs of those who were threatened.

Is an adaptation of this idea worth thinking about? Let's say that firings are imminent in your work group. Many may harbor the illusion of safety, figuring that they have seniority, or that they are too valuable to be let go, or that the boss is too nice a guy to do anything like that. But nobody really knows who will feel the ax, or how many.

Under such pressure you might try some informal talk with your colleagues about a plan that could save everyone's job. Consider the possibilities of giving up vacations, or overtime, or voluntarily guaranteeing increases in productivity. Some will resist, obviously, but if you get enough worried people to go along, you may have something with which to approach the bosses.

The boss may be in such a bind that he will have to let some workers go anyway—but such an approach might well cut down the number of layoffs. This display of willingness might imbue management with the feeling that it should explore every possibility of avoiding layoffs. Certainly this kind of offer—if based on solid guarantees, not just airy conversation—will open up avenues of dialogue with the boss that can lead to job-saving solutions.

This involves giving up something. You may have to work longer hours at lower pay. But if it works, you will still be receiving a paycheck. And you will probably continue to enjoy something more important: the opportunity to receive fringes like health insurance at lower cost or no cost at all. The sudden necessity to pay private rates for health coverage is one of the most traumatic results of unemployment for a lot of people. (In fact the fringes may be one fruitful area of compromise with the boss. If he is like most employers these fringes are running him about thirty percent of his payroll cost, and he may feel he is receiving little in the way of credit or additional effort for his expenditure. If, for example, a group of employees agrees to pay part of a fringe package, which was previously carried in toto by the company, there may well be an opportunity to save jobs.)

You can't lose much by trying to organize such an effort. True, there are apt to be a few colleagues who will look at you askance and mumble things about kowtowing to the bosses. But you're likely to find even more colleagues who are worried enough about their jobs to be willing to at least explore ways to hang in there.

Finally, even if the effort fails, your image in the eyes of management as the person who tried to find a workable alternative can be extremely helpful. When the time comes to make up the cut list, the employer may be reluctant to dispense with someone who has shown resourcefulness and a certain amount of sympathy with management problems.

Purposeful Friendship

One of the staples of reform movements in politics is chronic outrage at the fact that politicians tend to appoint their friends to jobs. Many of us would agree, objectively, that there is something unfair about this, but most of us have come to take it for granted. After all, we tell ourselves, politicians are human. Should they be expected to appoint their enemies?

Bosses are as human as politicians. Yet they are not *supposed* to let friendship color their decisions. The books and training manuals do not approve of this practice. And yet it goes on. Bosses are not often able to totally ignore the pull of friendship, particularly when it comes to personnel decisions. Of course, this may, on occasion, work to the detriment of the manager's friend, particularly if the friendship is widely known. The boss may feel compelled to lean over backward to avoid the appearance of playing favorites. However, by and large it is better to be the boss's friend.

If you are friendly with your boss and you see a crunch coming, you can best take advantage of that personal tie by soft-pedaling it. Don't put your boss on the spot of having to rule against you because of the implications of a favorable decision. On the job be all business. Refrain from seeking out the boss and flaunting your cordial relationship. Maintain off-the-job ties, but keep them away from the work site. And don't initiate conversations about who's going to keep his job and who will be laid off. If your friendship is solid, you can be reasonably sure you'll get every possible break. If you seem to be pushing it, your insistence could be counterproductive, both to the relationship and to your job-keeping prospects.

But let's assume you are not a particular friend of the boss's. Maybe it's time to think about becoming one.

A lot of managers appear not to have any friends among those who report to them. Subordinates frequently assume that this kind of boss does not want friends in the ranks. But that may not be the case. It may be that the boss would welcome some human give-and-take with one of the gang. But he shies away from making overtures, either because he does not know how to go about it or he fears rejection. (Yes, bosses are hurt by rejection just like everybody else.) An altruistic effort on your part to offer the hand of friendship and thus ease some of the lonely burden of command, may chalk up future points for you in heaven and also work to your advantage right here on earth.

Dan Millington works for Herb Luce. Luce has always been an aloof guy. He is civil enough, and he is fair. But nobody has ever seen him go out of his way to be cordial. The people who work for Luce consider him a cold fish.

Millington shares this opinion. But Millington has things on his mind. There have been layoffs in other areas of the company. So far his area has been untouched. Nevertheless Dan is worried. He looks around for angles. And one of the things that occurs to him is that he might want to get to know the boss a little better.

Dan Millington waits for an opportunity; in fact, he makes the opportunity. Luce usually leaves the job after almost everyone else has gone. One evening Millington waits around and "finds himself" on the same elevator with the boss. They exchange a couple of remarks. Then Millington says, "I was figuring on having a beer before going home. Want to join me?" Dan can't lose anything by asking. The worst that can happen is that Luce will say no.

But Luce doesn't say no. He harrumphs a little, then replies, "Why, yeah, I wouldn't mind a beer. Give us a chance to talk a little about those orders that will be coming in from Houston next week." (Sometimes when initiating a social contact with a "cold fish" boss, it's a good idea to suggest that there is a work-related angle to it. In this case the boss provided the pretext himself, but Dan Millington might have been prepared to do so himself.)

Over a beer the conversation is not sparkling, but Herb Luce gradually relaxes. Most of the talk is shoptalk, but they get around to exchanging data about wives, kids, houses, cars, and the high cost of living. The one thing that Dan Millington does *not* bring up is the economic situation of the company and the possibility of layoffs. This would have been a giveaway. Although it must be added that, while Millington has a distinct motive of survival in cultivating his boss, he is a friendly guy and is rather enjoying getting to know Luce as a human being.

In the weeks that follow Millington pursues the friendship. Meanwhile the likelihood of firings seems to be getting closer. And at last Dan concludes that it's time to raise the subject during one of these social occasions. Indeed it would begin to seem awkward if he did not raise it.

Millington picks his moment and comes out with it: "I think it's great the way you've been able to keep the whole outfit hanging in there, Herb, but I guess you must be as worried as the rest of us about the situation."

After a pause Luce admits he is somewhat concerned. Millington says some things about how much the job means to him. Luce offers no guarantees, but Millington comes away feeling that he has probably helped himself in the struggle to stay on the job. Certainly his friendship with the boss will not hurt him.

The more friendless and aloof your boss seems, the better may be the opportunity to use this approach. Just arrange an opportunity to get to know him better. Keep it casual; let him turn it down if he wants to. And when talking on relaxed terms with the boss, don't bring up job tenure right away. Wait until your acquaintanceship has had a chance to ripen a bit.

This is, admittedly, a somewhat calculating way to make friends. But that doesn't mean that a lasting friendship—as well as a tightened grip on the job—will not grow out of it. We all pick our friends for some reason. Continued employment rates as a respectable basis for broadening your social circle to include the boss.

Ask for a Break

In Arthur Miller's prize-winning play, *Death of a Salesman,* there is a poignant scene in which Willy Loman goes to the boss to beg for his job. The boss is the son of the employer who hired Willy and with whom the aging salesman worked for many years.

Willy is desperate; and yet he cannot bring himself to

make a simple plea for mercy. The new employer is portrayed as such a louse that probably nothing would help. Nevertheless Willy's effort is an object lesson in how *not* to do it. Willy struts. He recalls past triumphs. He engages in phony chitchat while the obviously busy boss fidgets impatiently. Willy acts at times as if he is doing the boss a favor. And he blusters about how "promises were made in this office." Needless to say Loman gets no place with all this.

Let's face it. Asking for sympathy is tough. Throwing yourself on the boss's mercy is a measure of desperation. But you may find yourself desperate enough to do it. This is nothing to be ashamed of. The individual who can nerve himself up to do what's necessary—distasteful as it may be—has more moral courage than the person who is willing to court extreme hardship for himself and his family because he "will not lower himself to beg."

If you wind up in such a fix, up against the need to try to win the boss's sympathy, you might as well do it right.

When an employee asks the boss to "have a heart," the first basic requirement is that the boss possess a heart that can be had. Some people assume that certain managers are altogether dry of the milk of human kindness. But most bosses, even the toughest, have hearts. Even the most seemingly Scroogelike supervisor can turn out to be willing to give somebody a break—if he finds it possible to do so.

You'll want to be sure that the situation is sufficiently desperate before you ask for the boss's sympathy. But since this is such a hard thing to do, it is not likely that you will bite the bullet and attempt it unless the situation is critical. The big thing is not to wait until you are actually fired. You have a chance, slim though it may be, if you are imploring the boss *before* he lowers the boom. If he has already said the fateful words "We're going to have to let you go," you don't have a chance. Once he has nerved himself up to do it—and for most bosses it's not at all easy—he is not going to reverse his decision. Your supplications will be futile and will just leave a bad taste in your mouth to cap off your other woes.

Pick a time when the boss is not under pressure. He is not going to enjoy the conversation; don't make it easy for him to brush you off with the excuse—made to himself as much as to you—that he is too busy to talk. You will not get another chance.

Don't muddy up your plea with *machismo*, and don't talk in code. Make it plain: "I know that some people are going to be laid off and I'm worried sick about it. My wife has not been well, and we've had some big bills with the kids. If I'm out of a job I just don't know what I'll do. You know I've always done my best for you. Am I going to be laid off?"

If he says you're not, you can go away with at least that assurance. But the boss will probably hedge. You don't really expect guarantees. Frankly your purpose at that moment is to lay it on as thick as possible in an effort to influence his sympathies in your behalf. Don't get hysterical, but tell him how much you are depending on the job. But don't leave it at that. Add the assurance of your gratitude and your loyalty if you get to keep the job: "If it's possible for you to keep me on I will never forget it. If there's anything I can do that will help you and help me keep the job, please tell me."

This last is important. You are asking him to tell you what you have to do to keep the job. If the boss picks up this gambit, he is not likely to talk about the impossible. Try to get him to focus on some aspect of the job that needs improvement—something that is at least possible. Then go away and do your damndest to accomplish what he asked.

Then report back to him later with evidence that at least you have given it an outstanding try.

The point of this approach is that you are combining a plea for a break with two other elements: the pledge that you will respond loyally and gratefully, and the dedication to do anything within reason to keep the job. There are times when this is enough to save the situation.

The Threat of Disruption

Al Brent has been talking with his boss, Frank Bloom, about some changes in the job. But now Brent takes off on a different tack: "Frank, the natives are getting restless." Bloom asks what he means. Brent answers, "The boys are pretty nervous. They think a lot of us are going to get fired. I've been putting my neck on the block telling them they're full of it. I said to one guy today—I won't mention who it is—'Do you think I'd be going along here, doing my job, cooperating every way I can, if I thought the outfit was going to throw any of us out of work without warning?' I got them calmed down, but people are wondering."

Bloom makes a noncommittal response; Brent doesn't expect any more. A few days later Al Brent returns to the topic, this time with an additional twist: "You know, Frank, things are tense. The lid could blow off this place if people start getting laid off. You know me, I don't let these things bother me. I just do my job and tell the other guys to hang in there and do theirs. Of course I'm taking it for granted that everything's going to be OK, and that none of us guys who have sunk our lives into this company are going to have the rug pulled out from under us. To tell you the truth, anything like that would make me real bitter, and I wouldn't care who knew it. But I know damn well we can count on you to keep the team together—or to let us know in plenty of time if there're going to be people fired."

To this Frank Bloom says, "You know, Al, I'm not a magician. I can't read the future. All I can tell you is that things look OK at the moment." Al Brent nods, "I'll take your word for that, Frank. And I know you can't work miracles. If somebody has to be let go, you'll be fair about it."

There are more such exchanges. You can see what Al Brent is doing. He's applying veiled blackmail. In effect he is saying, "If you fire me I will not take it like a gentleman. I will do everything I can to spread disruption and disaffection to everybody who stays on the payroll. So if you don't want to have hell raised with your operation, you had better keep me around." In the parlance of the Godfather, Al Brent hopes he is making the boss "an offer he can't refuse."

This does not cement friendships between bosses and subordinates. It is not a pleasant tactic. But sometimes it works. There may be other people in Bloom's group who possess at least as much potential for damage as does Brent, but they haven't expressed it. Bloom *knows* that Al Brent will be vindictive if he is fired and will try to do as much harm as he can before going. Furthermore Bloom is aware of how much damage a disgruntled ex-employee can do, even in the few hours it takes to get him off the premises. And it wouldn't end there. There is nothing to keep Al Brent from coming around to meet his old buddies and spread sedition.

If you feel the situation calls for such a tough measure, you may decide to put this sort of pressure on your boss. Don't come right out and say that you will try to make things tough if you are let go. Imply it by stressing how hard you are working to reassure your colleagues, adding that you would be burned up, indeed, if you were to be fired, but you know it won't come to that.

Of course you may be fired anyway. If that happens, should you carry through on the threat? No. In fact you can point out that you were tempted to, but that you decided against it. The boss, relieved somewhat, may look more sympathetically on the possibility of rehiring you when things pick up and will probably be more accommodating about references when you look for another job.

The potency of this technique lies in the threat, not the actuality. It is an extreme measure, but that is what we are talking about here—extremes.

So far in this chapter we have not explored such far-out possibilities as seduction, bribery, or threat of bodily harm. The last method we outlined involves a form of blackmail, but not the kind that constitutes a crime.

Actually the list of extreme measures is limited by two things, your *imagination* and the *law*. For example, here is another group of moves you can make or pressures you can exert, which, in a last-ditch stand, can turn the tide in your favor:

• *Owe the firm money.* Can this approach work? Listen:

"That assistant headwaiter of yours doesn't seem to add much to this operation," a friend tells a restaurant owner. "With things so tight, why do you keep him on?"

"He's into the company for about three thousand dollars on a personal loan. A stupid situation, I know, but if we fire him we'll never see that cash again."

The financial obligation can be to the company, your boss, or perhaps some other highly placed executive. In any event, it's obvious that if your source of income is removed, chances for collecting are zero.

• *Make the boss personally obligated.* How far you go or what is involved depends on the individual situation. But let us remind you of the popular comedy, *The Apartment,* starring Jack Lemmon, which had audiences rolling in the aisles. Behind the comedy lay a basic fact: An employee curries favor with his boss and other executives in the company by making his bachelor apartment available to them for their liaisons. Their gratitude is expressed in the form of raises and promotions.

• *Would demoralization follow your being fired?* Some individuals, because of personal popularity or other special qualifications, become important to the company image. In one company a well-known sports figure was hired as an adjunct to the personnel department and its recreation program. When business soured, the football player was called in to be told the bad news.

"I'd think twice before laying me off," he told his boss. "Maybe I shouldn't say it myself, but I'm a key figure here, and if I'm fired you'll really push the panic button for a lot of people."

There's just enough truth in the likelihood of a general demoralization that follows the firing of a popular organizational figure to use it as a reminder if the situation arises.

• *Who do you know?* The old apple about *it's not what you know but who you know* doesn't have to be argued here. But there's no question that friendships you have anywhere in the upper echelons can be a favorable factor. If the threat of a layoff hangs over you, consider calling on anyone you know up the ladder who can throw some weight on the scales. Make it quite clear what you hope for: "Tom, I'd appreciate it if you saw Mr. Miller and say whatever you can to get him to keep me on. . . ."

When you are desperate to keep your job, you will be tempted to use extreme approaches. They may be long shots, but they can lower the odds somewhat. However, they won't do anything for you if you don't employ them effectively. Any method, extreme or otherwise, should be pursued with planning and determination.

13

Putting It All Together—
Your Job Strategy

T̲ʜᴇ preceding chapters have presented you with a variety
of tactics. Put them together in the proper mix to form a
strategy for keeping your job and strengthening your career
in your organization.

As you review the tactics we've described, you'll find that
some don't seem to fit your job circumstances. Forget about
these and work with the rest.

In considering those tactics that might be applied, you
will react to each approach in a different way. For
example, you may look over one tactic and conclude that,
while it may be of use in maintaining your grip on the job,
it will do nothing else for you. It will not make you a more
effective performer. However, you may size up another
tactic and decide that it has two facets: It will strengthen
your hold on employment *and* it will enable you to be a
better worker.

The optimum category will contain tactics that offer four

advantages: They help you to keep your job; they enhance your ability; they improve your promotability or actually advance you in the organization; *and you feel good about them*.

These are the ploys that you will find easy to put into operation and that will add to your enjoyment of life on the job. For instance, you may have wished for some time that you could work closely with the boss in learning how to perform your job better. For various reasons you have not made any overtures to the boss. For one thing you worry about what your colleagues will think and whether they will say that you are toadying to authority. Now with the added pressure of job insecurity, you decide to do it. You get to know the boss better, you learn new things that enable you to work easier and more effectively, and you like the new relationship.

When you identify a tactic that fills the bill in these four ways: strengthened hold on the job, improved effectiveness, increased promotability, greater enjoyment—put it into operation immediately. You will handle it well, and it's something you should be doing anyway.

As for the other available approaches, give higher priority to those that make you a better performer as well as a more secure jobholder. However, as you assess the job situation (Chapter Three) you may decide that you must resort to certain tactics that have no dimension except that of job security.

As you do this—that is, assess various moves—you will be putting together a strategy.

Sometimes we tend to think of *strategy* as an extremely complex operation indulged in by generals and big-time politicians. Not so. We are all strategists. Those who have the advantage are the people who *know* that certain situations call for strategy, who think in strategic terms, and who go about getting what they want more systematically.

The elements of strategy—that is, a planned overall program aimed toward a given target—are basically simple. They comprise: setting the objective, marshalling resources, outlining alternative methods for attaining the objective, choosing the best alternative, putting the plan into effective operation.

In the context of this book the first element of strategy is clear. Your main objective is to keep your job. There are subsidiary objectives: to enhance your performance, to speed your growth, to enjoy your working life more. But the *main* goal is clear.

This fact simplifies your strategic thinking. Strategists in many areas come to grief on that first point: They can't define the main objective properly. This is not your problem.

Marshal your resources. The suggestions and questions in the early part of this book will help you to see more clearly the situation you are in, and to identify the strengths—potential and actual—that you have going for you. In general you'll be asking yourself:

- How do I stand with the boss? With the company?
- What do they see as my strong points? My weak points?
- What are the most effective things I might do to tighten my hold on the job?
- What are my capabilities and deficiencies? How do they fit the things I have to do?

Take an inventory of yourself: your personality, your experience, your length of time on the job, your relationships with others, your ability. These are the resources you will call upon to put together your strategy.

Outline alternative methods. In this step you will compose more than one possible strategy for yourself. You may work them out in your head, or you may want to sketch them in writing.

At this stage you don't have to be cautious. Be bold. Speculate on the more far-out plans as well as the more conservative ones. The idea is to be able to look at a number of possible strategies and then pick the best one; or to pick elements from several of the projected strategies and combine them in your ultimate grand design.

Choose the best alternative. The optimum strategy may not be the one that looks the best on paper. For example, as you compare them, it may appear that the best bet is to get really close to your own boss. Objectively it might look as if this strategy holds the maximum promise.

But you don't feel comfortable with this approach. Maybe you can't stand the boss. Maybe others are so close to him that you would be trying to penetrate a closed circle. So, instead, you go for a strategy that involves making yourself indispensable, whatever the relationship with the boss may be. This latter approach may offer less potential results in the abstract, but may be more doable in the light of all the considerations.

In considering which is the best strategy, think about possible side effects. How about the future? For instance, a strategy of total commitment to the current manager of a department might hold the best short-run promise for holding on to the job. However, this particular boss might be close to retirement, and obvious adherence to him might compromise your chances for promotion when the new head takes over. You will have to evaluate any plan in the light of *all* its ramifications, and you may have to make trade-offs between security now and growth later.

Put your plan into operation. The strategy you select

should not be just an attractive dream. It should contain at least one tactic that you can begin to work on immediately. No strategy is worth anything unless it is carried through.

Keeping your job is not a matter of luck. And sometimes, unfortunately, it is more than a matter of merely plugging away and hoping that your performance will carry you through. Job retention requires that you do your best and do it reasonably well; but there are other angles to be considered.

In this book we have tried to take a cool, objective look at those other angles and to suggest plans that will help you in your continuing quest for the paycheck. Good luck for a long and happy life—on the job!